The Young Astronomer's Handbook

Published 1984 by Arco Publishing, Inc.
215 Park Avenue South, New York, NY 10003
© Copyright The Hamlyn Publishing Group Limited 1981

Library of Congress Cataloging in Publication Data

Ridpath, Ian.
  The young astronomer's handbook

  Includes index.
  Summary: An illustrated guide to astronomy with
information on astronomical instruments, the solar
system, the celestial sphere, the origins of the
universe, and theories of astronomy from ancient times to
the present. Also includes a section on constellations
pointing out objects of interest that can be observed
with simple equipment.
  1. Astronomy—Juvenile literature. [1. Astronomy]
I. Title.
QB46.R545 1984   520   83-15701
ISBN 0-668-06046-8

Printed in Italy

The Young Astronomer's Handbook

Ian Ridpath

ARCO PUBLISHING, INC.
New York

Acknowledgements

Photographs

Ron Arbour, Bishopstoke 48, 49 top, 49 bottom, 50, 55, 174, 175; Archives Photographiques, Paris 9; Bell Laboratories, Murray Hill, New Jersey 211; Biblioteca Marucelliana, Florence 22; Bord Failte/Irish Tourist Board, Dublin 38; British Museum, London 69; California Institute of Technology and the Carnegie Institute of Washington. Reproduced by permission from the Hale Observatories, Pasadena 33 bottom, 40 bottom left, 41, 72, 84, 86, 102, 105 bottom, 120, 122 bottom, 133 bottom, 135 bottom, 138, 145, 151, 153, 180 top, 192; A. P. Dowdell, Winchester 194; Storm Dunlop, East Wittering 81, 140 left, 141; Mary Evans Picture Library, London 14, 21, 27 top, 28 bottom, 39 top; David Gavine, Edinburgh 162 top; Griffith Observatory, Los Angeles – Lois Cohen 89; Hamlyn Group Picture Library 15, 17, 18, 20, 23 top, 27 bottom, 34, 196 bottom; Hansen Planetarium, Salt Lake City 110, 137, 165, 213; Michael Holford Library, Loughton 8 top, 24, 35 bottom, 36 right; Kitt Peak National Observatory, Tucson 61 bottom, 63, 65 top, 65 bottom, 73, 105 top, 117, 124, 129, 148; Lick Observatory, University of California, Santa Cruz 61 top, 79, 88, 112, 122 top, 135 top; Los Alamos Scientific Laboratory, New Mexico 196 top; Robert McNaught, Prestwick 66-67; Mount Wilson Observatory, Pasadena 136; Mullard Radio Astronomy Observatory, Cambridge 45 left; NASA, Washington, D.C. 33 top, 44 bottom, 45 right, 90, 92-93, 127, 155, 159, 162 bottom, 163 top, 163 bottom, 167, 170, 171, 172, 176, 177, 178, 179 top, 179 bottom, 180 bottom, 182, 183, 184, 185 top, 185 bottom, 186 top, 186 bottom, 187, 188, 189, 190, 199, 200, 201, 202 top, 202 centre, 202 bottom, 203, 204; National Maritime Museum, London 19 top; National Portrait Gallery, London 25 top, 28 top; Novosti Press Agency, London 40 top right; Col. A. Page, Brisbane 119; Walter Pennell, Lincoln 107; H. B. Ridley, Yeovil 104; Ian Ridpath, London, 40 top left; Ann Ronan Picture Library, Loughton 19 bottom; Royal Greenwich Observatory, Herstmonceaux 161; Royal Observatory, Edinburgh 113, 128, 144; Robin Scagell, Uxbridge 6; Science Museum, London: Crown Copyright 35 top; Smithsonian Astrophysical Observatory, Massachusetts 40 bottom right; Space Frontiers, Havant 111, 115 bottom, 123, 152, 197, 204-205; Tony Stone Associates, London title page, 8; United States Naval Observatory, Washington, D.C. 32, 64; University of Michigan 42; Roger-Viollet, Paris 70; Von Del Chamberlain, Washington, D.C. 130, 146, 150; Dr James D. Wray, Austin, Texas 130, 131, 154; Yerkes Observatory, Wisconsin 23 bottom, 31, 39 bottom; Z.E.F.A., London – Gunter Heil 36 left; Z.E.F.A. – Gerolf Kalt 44 top.

Front jacket – main picture Space Frontiers, Havant; top inset Science Museum, London; bottom insets, right Ron Arbour, Bishopstoke; left, Smithsonian Astrophysical Observatory, Massachusetts.

Back jacket – top left Dr James D. Wray, Austin, Texas; top right NASA, Washington, D.C.; bottom ZEFA, London

Research in the USA by Frances C. Rowsell, Washington, D.C.

Illustrations

David A. Hardy 25 bottom, 43 top, 160; David Lewis Artists; The Tudor Art Agency Limited.

Contents

Introduction

Astronomy has rightly been called the oldest of the sciences. It began in the mists of prehistory when people gazed in uncomprehending awe at the Sun, the Moon, the stars, and the planets. The Universe still holds many mysteries for us, but astronomers have made considerable progress in understanding the objects around us in Space.

You can start to find your way around the sky with nothing more than your own eyes, and perhaps a pair of binoculars. You don't need a telescope to become an astronomer, although all beginners ultimately aspire to owning a telescope that will reveal some of the details of the Universe that are beyond the reach of the naked eye. This book sets out to explain what the objects are that you can see in the sky, and how astronomers have found out about them. A major feature of the book is the section describing each constellation in detail, pointing out the objects of interest for amateur observers with simple equipment. All the information given in this book is relevant to both northern and southern hemispheres, except where indicated otherwise.

With the advent of the space age, astronomy has become an exciting science of exploration and discovery. For young and old, astronomy is one of the most mind-expanding of all interests. Anyone who reads this book can truly say they have been introduced to the Universe!

Ian Ridpath

Early views of the Universe

Ancient peoples knew more about the sky than we often realize. They observed the passage of the Sun, Moon and stars in order to make calendars, so that they would know when to sow, reap, and to celebrate religious festivals. One of the most accurate early calendars was that of the ancient Egyptians at least 2000 years BC. They based their calendar on observations of the sky's brightest star, Sirius, which they called Sothis. Circles of standing stones, found in northern Europe and elsewhere, are aligned unmistakably with the rising and setting points of the Sun and Moon. Most famous and sophisticated of these circles is Stonehenge in

Above: Nut, the Egyptian sky goddess, surrounded by figures of the Zodiac, painted on the inside of a coffin lid.

Below: Stonehenge is believed to have been an observatory for following the motions of the Sun and Moon.

England, the oldest part of which was constructed about 2500 BC. Stonehenge was evidently used as an observatory for following the motions of the Sun and Moon; it may even have served as a kind of computer for predicting eclipses.

Rise of modern astronomy

Modern astronomy began about 600 BC with the Greeks, who built upon the earlier knowledge of the Egyptians and other middle-eastern peoples. One of their earliest, and most important, discoveries was that the Earth is not flat. Anyone who travels far in the northern hemisphere soon realizes that the Earth's surface must be curved, because the altitude of the Pole Star (Polaris) changes when seen from different latitudes. Anaximander (circa 610-

546 BC), a Greek philosopher who is sometimes called the father of astronomy, believed the Earth was a cylinder curving from north to south. But soon it became clear to mariners and others that the Earth is curved in all directions, not just from north to south. In other words, it must be a sphere.

Aristotle (384-322 BC), a leading Greek philosopher, knew that the Earth and also the Moon are spherical in shape, but he did not realize that the Earth rotates. Instead, he believed that the Earth lay stationary at the centre of the Universe, with all else moving around it on transparent crystalline spheres. He used a system of 55 spheres to account for the observed motions of the Sun, Moon, planets and stars. This idea of the heavenly spheres took root in astronomical thought, and was not finally banished until 2000 years after Aristotle.

Below: The Earth was visualized as a cylinder by the Greek philosopher Anaximander in the 6th century BC.

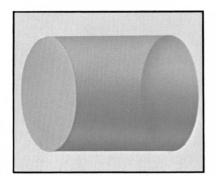

Below: Aristotle was a Greek philosopher who believed that celestial bodies circled the Earth on transparent spheres.

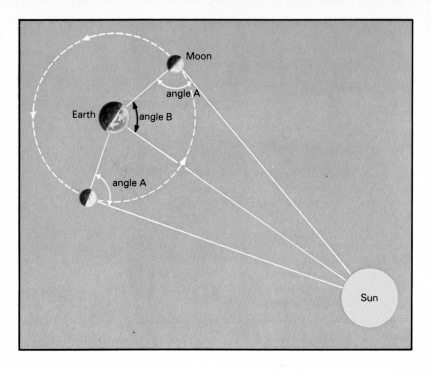

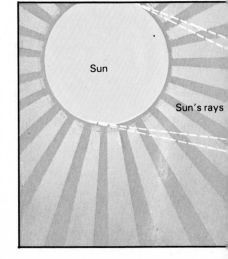

Aristarchus measures the Sun and Moon

Around 270 BC the Greek astronomer Aristarchus attempted to measure the relative distances of the Sun and Moon by an ingenious method, as shown in the diagram. This is how he went about it. When the Moon is exactly half illuminated as seen from Earth, the Moon forms a right angle (90°) with the Earth and Sun (angle A). Aristarchus attempted to measure the angle (angle B) between the Moon and the Sun at this moment and found it to be 87°. Aristarchus worked out that the distance from the Earth to the Sun in this triangle is

Left: How the Greek scientist Aristarchus tried to calculate the relative distances of the Sun and Moon, using trigonometry.

about 19 times the distance of the Earth to the Moon. In reality, the Sun is about 400 times farther away than the Moon. The large error arose because angle B is difficult to measure accurately, but despite this considerable underestimate Aristarchus was at least on the right track.

Aristarchus next tried to measure the relative sizes of the Sun, Earth, and Moon by a simple method which anyone (with a little ingenuity) can duplicate today. Begin by choosing any point as the centre of the Earth. During a lunar eclipse the Sun and Moon are in a straight line with the Earth, but on opposite sides of it. The Sun and Moon appear to us to be the same size in the sky – approximately half a degree across – although the Sun is 19 times farther away (by Aristarchus' estimate) than the Moon. Therefore, draw two lines, intersecting at an angle of half a degree, through the point representing the centre of the Earth. On one side, between these lines, draw in a circle to represent the Moon. On the opposite side, 19 times farther away from the point, draw in the Sun.

This is the situation that exists at the time of a lunar eclipse (when the Earth blocks off the Sun's light from the Moon). From observations made at eclipses, the size of the Earth's shadow that fell on the Moon was estimated as 2·7 times the size of the Moon. This shadow can be drawn in

Below: Aristarchus attempted to measure the relative sizes of the Sun, Earth and Moon with the aid of a simple scale drawing like the one below.

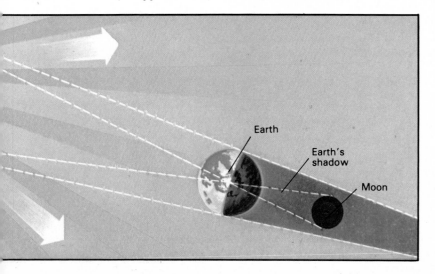

Earth

Earth's shadow

Moon

Above: Earth and Moon shown relative to a segment of the Sun. The Moon's diameter is a quarter of the Earth's: the Sun's diameter is over 100 times the Earth's

around the Moon on the diagram, and from it two lines can be drawn to the edges of the Sun's disc. These lines must touch the edges of the Earth – so the Earth can now be filled in on the drawing and the relative sizes of the Sun and Moon in terms of the Earth's diameter can be read off.

Although this is no easy construction to perform, with its long lines and small angles, the principle is simple enough to follow. From his own figures, Aristarchus found that the Moon is about one-third the size of the Earth, which is not far from being accurate (the true figure is one-quarter). He estimated the Sun to be seven times larger than the Earth, which is a gross underestimate – the Sun is actually 109 times the Earth's diameter. This was due to the error in his estimation of the Sun's distance

from Earth. But he had at least discovered that the Sun is a larger body than the Earth, which was support for his theory that the Sun was the centre of the Universe, with the Earth and other celestial objects orbiting it. Alas, his views about the arrangement of the planets were not accepted by other astronomers, who relied instead on the erroneous theory of Aristotle, that the Earth lay at the centre of the Universe.

Eratosthenes measures the Earth

The Greeks now had several distances in terms of the Earth's diameter. But what is the Earth's diameter?

Moon

Eratosthenes worked out that answer in 240 BC. He noted that at noon on a particular day the Sun lies directly overhead at Syene, Egypt (near modern Aswan). But at the same time at Alexandria, 800 kilometres farther north, the Sun lies about 7° from the vertical – the reason being the curvature of the Earth. Since 7° is roughly one-fiftieth of a circle (360°), it follows that the circumference of the Earth must be 50 times the distance from Alexandria to Syene. On this basis, Eratosthenes calculated that the Earth has a

Below: Eratosthenes, a Greek scientist, worked out the size of the Earth very accurately around 240 BC.

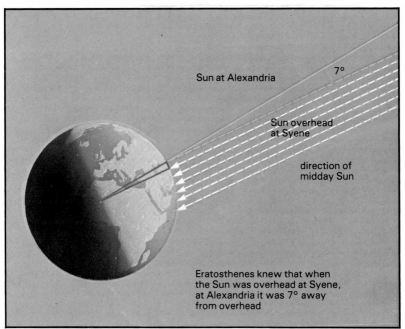

Sun at Alexandria   7°

Sun overhead at Syene

direction of midday Sun

Eratosthenes knew that when the Sun was overhead at Syene, at Alexandria it was 7° away from overhead

circumference of approximately 40000 kilometres – an accurate result. It seems odd, therefore, that 1700 years later Columbus thought the Earth to be only half its true size!

Hipparchus, the great Greek astronomer.

Hipparchus, a great Greek observer

Outstanding among Greek astronomers was Hipparchus (who produced most of his observations from 146-127 BC), the greatest observer of ancient times. He made accurate observations of the apparent motion of the Sun, Moon and planets, and produced a catalogue of the positions of 850 stars – all using simple sighting instruments, for this was long before the telescope was invented!

One of Hipparchus' important discoveries was that of precession (see page 56), which causes a systematic shift in the positions of stars with time. Hipparchus was also responsible for introducing the system of magnitudes for expressing the brightness of stars. In his catalogue, he classified stars into six brightness categories, from first magnitude (the brightest stars) to sixth magnitude (the faintest stars visible to the naked eye). In modified form, this magnitude system is still in use today.

Ptolemy's geocentric theory
The last great Greek astronomer was

14

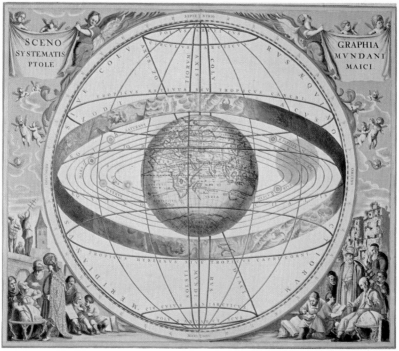

Ptolemy (circa AD 100-178) who wrote a major work on astronomy known to us as the 'Almagest', from the Arabic word meaning greatest. In the Almagest, Ptolemy put forward a detailed scheme with which he attempted to account for the observed motions of the Sun, Moon and planets, all of which he believed orbited the Earth, as Aristotle had stated.

Following the 'heavenly spheres' concept of Aristotle and others, the Greeks had come to believe that only the circle, being a 'perfect' figure, was suitable to describe the motions of

According to the Greek scientist Ptolemy in the second century AD, the Earth was the centre of the Universe, around which all other bodies revolved.

heavenly bodies. But it is obvious from the observed motions of the Sun, Moon and planets that they do not move in circular paths centred on the Earth. In particular, some planets move noticeably faster at some times than at others, or even seem to perform backward loop motions in the sky, as well as changing in brightness from one part of their orbit to another.

To explain the planets' behaviour,

15

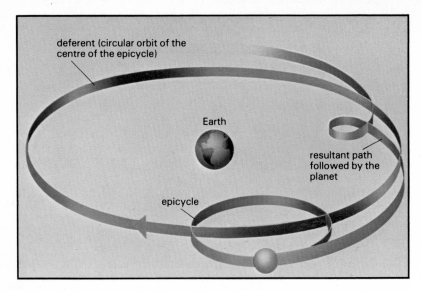

deferent (circular orbit of the centre of the epicycle)

Earth

resultant path followed by the planet

epicycle

Ptolemy used several devices (see above). Most important of these was the *epicycle*, a smaller circle centred on the rim of the main circular orbit (the *deferent*). The planet rode around the epicycle while the centre of the epicycle progressed smoothly along the deferent. This combination of motions could reproduce the apparent changes in speed and occasional loop movements of the planets. In addition, the centres of the deferents were offset from the centre of the Earth. And even this offset centre was imagined to travel around the Earth on a circular path known as the *eccentric*.

So Ptolemy piled wheel upon wheel to form a highly complex celestial clockwork. To us the system seems absurd. But the Earth-centred (geocentric) Universe as defined by

In Ptolemy's scheme, planets were thought to move in a small circle, an *epicycle*, on the rim of a larger circle, called the *deferent*, around the Earth.

Ptolemy, with its highly artificial combinations of gyrating circles, became the standard view of the Universe for 1300 years. Ptolemy and Aristotle were regarded as the ultimate authorities on astronomy until the 16th century.

After Ptolemy, astronomy went into a long period of stagnation. The Greek knowledge of astronomy was preserved by the Arabs, to whom we owe many of our modern star names, but they made few significant advances of their own. Eventually, though, a major challenger arose to the geocentric view of Ptolemy. This was the Sun-centred (heliocentric) theory of Nicolaus Copernicus.

Modern views of the Universe

Nicolaus Copernicus (1473-1543) was a Polish monk who caused a revolution in astronomy. It had become clear by his time that even the elaborate celestial clockwork of Ptolemy's geocentric system could not accurately represent the observed motions of the planets. Copernicus realized that it was logical to assume, as Aristarchus had done over 1700 years before him, that the Sun lay at the centre of the Universe, and that the Earth was an ordinary planet orbiting it.

Nicolaus Copernicus, the Polish astronomer who challenged centuries of dogma by proposing that the Sun, not the Earth, lay at the centre of the Universe.

In this arrangement, the different speeds of motion of the planets would be readily explained by their differing distances from the Sun, with the closest planets, Mercury and Venus, having the smallest orbits and moving the most swiftly, while the planets more distant than Earth – Mars, Jupiter, and Saturn (the outermost planet known at the time) – would have larger orbits and move more slowly. The perplexing 'loop' motion that planets occasionally performed was not due to any real reversal of their direction of travel at all, but simply an effect of their differing rela-tive speeds. As when one moving vehicle overtakes another, when the Earth passes a slower-moving planet, the slower planet appears to be moving backwards.

It all sounds delightfully simple, and in principle it is, for of course the planets actually do orbit the Sun, forming what is known as the Solar System. But Copernicus's heliocentric theory suffered from one major flaw. He was still shackled to the ancient principle that planetary

Copernicus placed the Sun at the centre of the Universe, with all else orbiting it.

motions must be expressed in combinations of circles. Consequently, his detailed construction of planetary motions became a maze of deferents and epicycles as complicated as that of Ptolemy, and scarcely any better for predicting the positions of the planets.

The theory of Copernicus was not, therefore, an overnight success, and received much criticism when it appeared in the book 'On the Revolutions of the Celestial Spheres' published in 1543, the year Copernicus died. The theory's importance was that it forced astronomers to look at the sky in a new way, which ultimately led to a breakthrough in our understanding of the Universe.

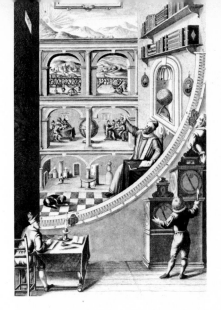

Above: Tycho Brahe, the Danish astronomer.

The observations of Tycho Brahe

Astronomers were hampered in their quest to explain the motions of the planets by a lack of precise observations of planetary positions. A Danish nobleman, Tycho Brahe (1546-1601), determined to remedy this defect. Tycho, as he is commonly called, was undoubtedly the greatest observer of pre-telescopic times. Among other achievements, he measured the length of the year to within one second, using sighting instruments larger and more accurate than any used before.

His observations of a 'new' star which appeared in 1572 (actually an old star flaring up in brightness as a supernova, see page 85) proved that this star was not, as some people had maintained, an effect in the atmosphere, but lay far off in space. This discovery invalidated the belief, commonplace since Greek times, that

Below: The 1572 supernova.

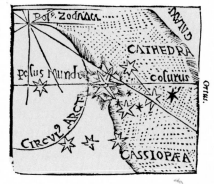

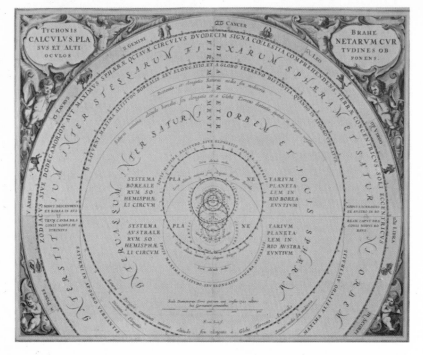

the heavens were perfect and unchanging. Further observations by Tycho of a comet which appeared in 1577 showed that this object moved on a path among the planets, underlining the fact that changes did occur in the heavens and finally shattering any remaining faith in the notion of solid crystalline spheres. The age-old authority of Aristotle, and hence the foundation of Ptolemy's geocentric theory, was severely damaged.

But what to put in its place? Tycho could not bring himself to support the heliocentric universe of Copernicus. Instead, he proposed a compromise system in which the planets, except

Tycho Brahe's view of the Universe.

the Earth, orbited the Sun, while the Sun in turn orbited a stationary, central Earth. On his death, Tycho bequeathed his 20 years of planetary observations to his assistant, a German mathematician named Johannes Kepler (1571-1630), in the hope that Kepler would use them to prove the Tychonic theory.

Kepler's laws

Instead, Kepler proved the heliocentric theory, that the Earth and other

Left: Johannes Kepler, †
mathematician who wo
of planetary motion.

metrical shape li
circle.)

Kepler's mathen
based on the precise ~~~~~~
Tycho, that the orbits of the planets
are ellipses, was published in 1609,
and is called 'Kepler's first law of
planetary motion'. It was a vital ad-
vance in banishing the outmoded and
restrictive Greek views of the heavens. Observation and calculation
had taken the place of dogma based
on ancient authorities.

Kepler also found that the planets
do not move along their elliptical
orbits at constant speed (another
overthrow of Greek views, which
held that planetary motions must be

planets orbit the Sun. And he made
one crucial discovery which over-
came the objections to Copernicus's
version of the theory. That discovery
was that the planets do not move in
combinations of circles. They move
in *ellipses.* (An ellipse is a simple geo-

Below: Kepler showed that planets move
fastest on their orbits when closest to the
Sun, and slowest when farthest away.

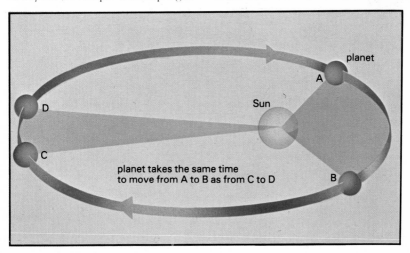

planet takes the same time
to move from A to B as from C to D

, but that a planet moves .n its orbit when closest to the , and slowest when farthest away. iis finding, when expressed in more precise terms, is Kepler's second law.

Kepler · continued his investigations, finding that a planet's orbital period is longer the farther the planet is from the Sun. This simple relationship between a planet's orbital period and its distance from the Sun enabled the calculation of the scale of the Solar System. This, Kepler's third law, was published in 1619. By then,

the observations of the Italian scientist Galileo Galilei (1564-1642) had established the truth of the heliocentric theory beyond doubt.

Galileo scans
the heavens

By one of those fortunate coincidences which abound in the history of

Galileo Galilei, the Italian scientist whose observations with a telescope brought about a revolution in astronomy.

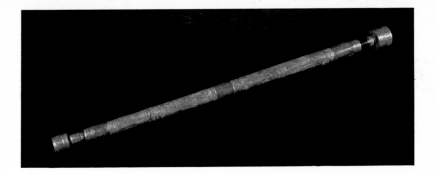

science, the telescope was just coming into use as Kepler announced his first two laws of planetary motion in 1609. In that same year, Galileo turned a small telescope of his own construction towards the sky and saw things that no man had seen before.

The surface of the Moon is not smooth and perfect as the ancient Greeks had maintained, but is rugged and mountainous. The planets Mercury and Venus are not perfectly rounded discs, and go through a cycle of phases similar to those shown by the Moon. The only explanation of this is that we must see different portions of those planets illuminated as they orbit the Sun, in confirmation of the theory of Copernicus.

Even more astounding, when Galileo looked at Jupiter he saw four satellites, which orbit it like a miniature version of the planets orbiting the Sun. And his telescopes brought into view countless faint stars, the existence of which had never been suspected by Aristotle and Ptolemy, thus totally and finally discrediting

Above: One of Galileo's telescopes, which he designed and built himself using spectacle lenses mounted in a tube. The telescope had a very low magnification.

the ultimate authority of the Greeks. The true nature of the heavens was visible to anyone who cared to look through a telescope.

Below: Galileo's drawings of mountains and craters on the surface of the Moon.

Newton and gravity

Once it had been established that the planets revolve around the Sun on elliptical orbits, the periods of which depend on their distance, it remained to be explained why they should move in this way. The great English scientist Isaac Newton (1642-1727) provided the explanation with his theory of gravity. This theory showed that each body attracts every other body with a force that depends on the masses of the bodies and their distance apart. (Mass is the measure of the quantity of matter, without any force of gravity acting upon it.) Since the Sun is the most massive body in the Solar System, it is natural that the planets should orbit it, rather than the much smaller Earth. Kepler's third law had already indicated that the force of gravity must decrease with distance, so that the outer planets are attracted less strongly, and move more slowly, than the inner planets. And a body moving under such an attraction would follow an elliptical path.

Newton's theory of gravity had many applications, such as explaining the cause of the tides, helping track the orbit of comets, and describing the motion of satellites around planets. Newton's theory has since been superseded by Einstein's theory of gravity, 'the general theory of relativity', which explains gravity in terms of the curvature of space; but for everyday purposes (including describing the motions of space probes) the laws of Newton are as valid as when he published them in his book 'Principia' in 1687.

Newton made several other important contributions to astronomy, notably by designing and building a new type of telescope known as a reflector, which uses a mirror to collect and focus light, unlike the spyglass type of telescope (a refractor) employed by other astronomers including Galileo, which uses lenses. Newton also found that sunlight could be split into its constituent colours (the rainbow band of the *spectrum*) by passing it through a prism. This was the first step in analysing light from celestial bodies to find their nature and composition, which led to the branch of astronomy called 'astrophysics'.

Above: Isaac Newton was perhaps the greatest scientist who ever lived.

Below: Newton split sunlight into its constituent colours using a prism.

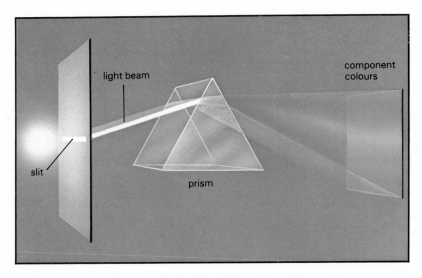

light beam

component colours

slit

prism

The scale of the Universe

In the span of a decade, Galileo and Kepler had confirmed that the Earth is a planet orbiting the Sun, and Kepler's laws had established a scale for the Solar System in terms of the Earth's distance from the Sun. But to calibrate the scale of the Solar System, astronomers still needed to know the exact distance of the Sun from the Earth. Some ingenious methods have been put to use.

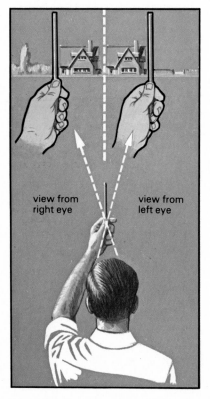

A pencil when viewed through first one eye and then the other shows a shift against the background, ie *parallax*.

view from right eye

view from left eye

The basic method of measuring distances in astronomy is that of *parallax*, the apparent change in position of an object as seen from two different places. For instance, a tree seems to move against the distant horizon as seen from two vantage points. The amount of position shift (parallax) depends on the tree's distance from the observer – the nearer the tree, the greater the change in position. Therefore the parallax of the tree enables its distance to be calculated. In the same way, the different positions of a planet against the background stars as seen from two different places on Earth enables its distance to be worked out. Once we know the distance of a planet from Earth at a set point in their two orbits, the scale of the entire Solar System follows, and hence the distance of the Earth from the Sun.

In 1672, the Italian-French astronomer Giovanni Domenico Cassini (1625-1712) worked out from observations of the parallax of Mars that the distance from the Earth to the Sun is 140 million kilometres – barely 10 million kilometres short of the true distance. But how far away are the stars?

Even before the time of Copernicus, it was realized that the stars are probably very much farther away than the Sun or planets, and it soon became clear that the stars are luminous bodies similar to the Sun, whereas

Above: Giovanni Domenico Cassini, the Italian astronomer who moved to France.

the middle of the 19th century direct parallaxes of several of the nearest stars had been obtained by measurements at six-month intervals, ie from opposite sides of the Earth's orbit (see also page 91). These results showed that even the nearest stars are so far away that their light takes several years to reach us. Distances in space are commonly expressed in light years, which is the distance covered by a beam of light in one year. A light year is equivalent to approximately 9·5 million million kilometres.

Below: Chinese star chart of circa 1700 AD. The Chinese used different constellations from ours, so stars are not immediately identifiable. However, the pale band of the Milky Way is easily recognized.

planets shine only by reflecting sunlight. In 1668 the Scottish astronomer James Gregory (1638-1675) estimated the distance of the star Sirius by comparing its brightness with that of the Sun, calculating it to be about 83 000 times farther away than the Sun (83 000 solar distances). Isaac Newton, in 1685, estimated Sirius to be at 950 000 solar distances. The true figure is 550 000 solar distances.

Despite the understandable inaccuracies in these figures (partly affected by the fact that Sirius is considerably brighter than the Sun), by the end of the 17th century astronomers had a reasonably good idea of the distance to the Sun and stars. And by

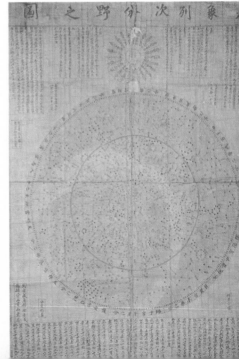

Above: Sir William Herschel was one of the outstanding observers of all time.

Below: Herschel's great reflector, over 12 metres long, was the largest telescope in the world when built in 1789.

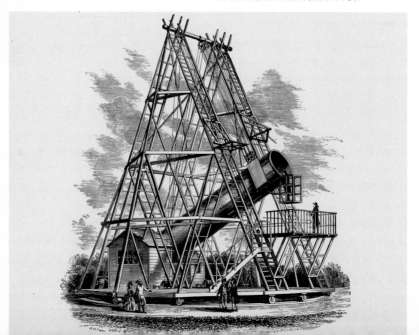

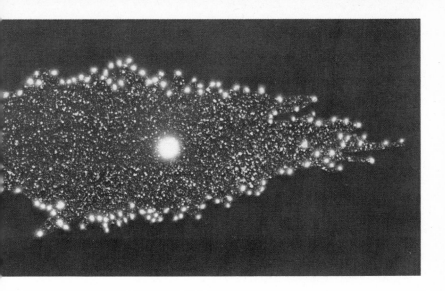

Our place in the Galaxy

Above: Herschel believed that the Galaxy was shaped like this, with the Sun (shown as a large white dot) near the centre.

Naturally, many questions remained. How far does the Universe extend? What else is contained in it? And where is the Sun situated? William Herschel (1738-1822), one of the greatest observers of all time, tried to find the answers. He surveyed over 600 selected areas of sky, using large reflecting telescopes of his own construction, and found that the stars are much more numerous in some directions (notably along the star-studded band of the Milky Way) than in others. He therefore concluded that the stars were arranged in a lens-shaped system, about five times as wide as it was thick, with the Sun approximately at the centre. He called this overall system of stars the Galaxy, and the Galaxy was assumed to be all that existed in the Universe – beyond was just empty space. This view was widely held even at the beginning of this century, when the Galaxy was thought to be about 55 000 light years in diameter and 11 000 light years thick.

Then came two revolutionary advances. The first was made by an American astronomer, Harlow Shapley (1885-1972) who showed in 1918 that the Sun does not lie at the centre of the Galaxy but in the galactic 'suburbs', thereby displacing the Sun from any privileged position in the Universe as firmly as Copernicus had previously displaced the Earth. Subsequently, another American

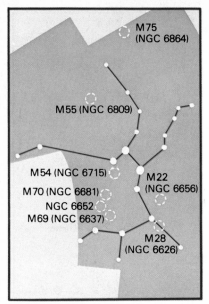

Left: The constellation Sagittarius (shown sideways). This diagram shows the location of its most prominent globular star clusters.

astronomer, Edwin Powell Hubble (1889-1953) showed that our Galaxy is not the only such star system in the Universe, but that Space is filled with countless other galaxies as far as telescopes could penetrate. Within the short span of about 10 years, the present view of the Universe became more or less established.

Shapley studied globular-shaped clusters (of which 125 have now been found) of stars and observed that they are not distributed randomly over the sky as one might have expected. Instead, most of them appeared to congregate in one region of sky, in the

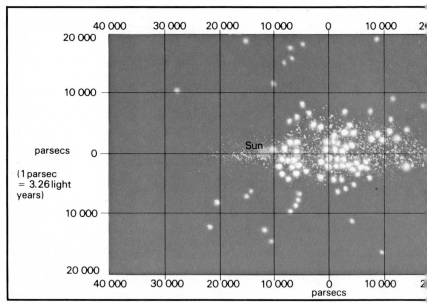

direction of the constellation Sagittarius. Shapley assumed, correctly as it turned out, that globular clusters are actually scattered more or less symmetrically around the hub of the Galaxy, and their apparent concentration in one direction is due to the fact that the Solar System is nowhere near the Galaxy's centre. On current estimates, the Galaxy is about 100 000 light years in diameter, and the Solar System lies about 30 000 light years from the centre.

Below: The distribution of globular star clusters within the Galaxy.

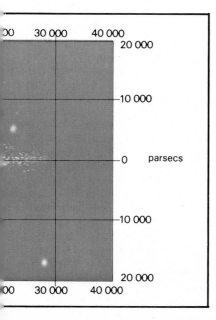

The Universe around us

This still left open the question of what, if anything, lies outside our Galaxy? The answer was soon forthcoming. Astronomers had long known of the existence of certain fuzzy patches in Space, called *nebulae* (singular: nebula) from the Latin word meaning cloud. Some of these nebulae–for instance, the famous nebula in Orion – obviously are glowing clouds of gas within the Galaxy. But others show a distinct spiral shape, and astronomers were far less sure about the nature of these. Some astronomers regarded the spiral nebulae as 'island universes', separate star systems like our own Galaxy, while others regarded them as aggregates of stars and gas within our Galaxy.

The controversy was resolved in 1923 when Edwin Hubble turned the 2·5-metre (100-inch) reflector on Mount Wilson, USA, then the world's largest telescope, towards the famous spiral nebula in Andromeda (see page 102), which is just visible to the naked eye. With this giant telescope, Hubble photographed individual stars in the nebula. Those stars were so faint he realized that the Andromeda 'nebula' must be far off in the Universe. It is, in fact, a separate spiral-shaped island, or galaxy, of stars like our own. According to latest measurements the Andromeda Galaxy is 2·2 million light years away, so that the light entering our eyes today actually left that galaxy 2·2 million years ago, when our ape-man ancestors were roaming the plains of Africa. The Andromeda Galaxy is the farthest object visible to the naked eye – but as galaxies go it is relatively close to us.

Hubble went on to study many more galaxies, classifying them according to their shape. Not only are there ordinary spirals, but there are elliptical galaxies, spirals with a bar of stars across the centre, and galaxies that are of such puzzling shape they can only be described as irregular.

The Orion Nebula is a glowing cloud of gas in our own Galaxy.

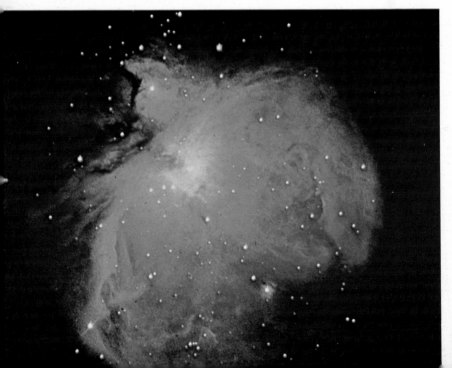

Right: M82 is an elongated, irregular galaxy which appears to be undergoing an explosion.

Then, in 1929, Hubble made an even more startling discovery. He found that all the galaxies appear to be rushing away from each other, as if the entire Universe were expanding like a balloon being blown up. Hubble's discovery of the expansion of the Universe is the starting point for modern theories of cosmology, which are discussed in more detail in the later chapter 'Beginnings and Endings'.

Below: The great spiral galaxy in Andromeda is a near twin of our own Milky Way. It is the most distant object visible to the naked eye.

Astronomical instruments

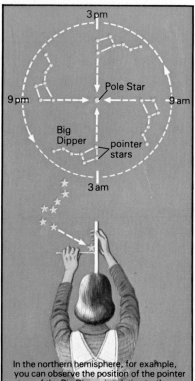

In the northern hemisphere, for example, you can observe the position of the pointer stars of the Big Dipper in relation to the Pole Star *(see page 152)* at night, and estimate their positions during the day. Then make a 24 hour disc (astrolabe) as shown above. Each quarter represents 6 hours. By comparing the angle you see between a line through the pointers and the Pole Star, and a ruler held vertical from the Pole Star's position, against your disc, you can estimate the time. In this example, it is 7pm (in January, since the constellation positions change through the year).

Above: Elegantly decorated Persian astrolabe of 1712 AD by Abd al A'imma.

Left: Making your own astrolobe to tell the time.

Early instruments

Before the invention of the telescope, astronomers were restricted to measuring the position of celestial objects by using simple sighting instruments.

The astrolabe

One such instrument is the astrolabe, which, in its simplest form, consists of

Above: An armillary sphere, an ancient instrument used for sighting on celestial objects.

time of night could be determined. In this form, the astrolabe served as a forerunner of the navigator's sextant.

The armillary sphere and the quadrant

A more complicated instrument was the armillary sphere, consisting of intersecting rings representing the horizon, ecliptic (see page 53), and the local meridian (the north-south line in the sky). Again, sighting on a celestial object allowed its celestial coordinates to be read off. Also frequently used was the quadrant, a quarter-circle graduated in degrees, with a movable sighting rod for reading off the altitude of stars. Tycho Brahe, the great Danish observer, brought this instrument to perfection by building quadrants larger and more accurate than any before.

a disc with a sight that could be pivoted to measure the altitude of an object. The Arabs made graduated astrolabes to show the altitudes of various bright stars at different times, so that by finding the right star the

Below: Mariner's quadrant, a forerunner of the sextant. Larger quadrants, mounted on walls for stability, were used by astronomers to measure star positions.

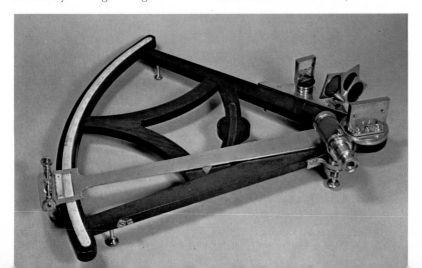

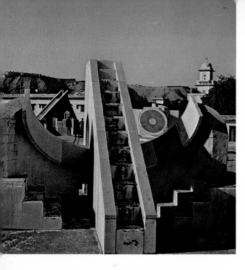

Above: Giant sundial made of stone, one of many instruments for observing the Sun's motion, erected by the Maharajah Jai Singh in 1734 at Jaipur, India.

Above: Portable telescope on an equatorial mounting, made by the English optician Jesse Ramsden (1735–1800).

The sundial

A sundial can also be regarded as a simple astronomical instrument. The Maharajah of Jaipur in India, Jai Singh II (1686-1743), built an amazing series of observatories using massive stone instruments for time-keeping purposes. (Note that Jai Singh's observatories used no optical instruments, even though the telescope had been in use for over a century when they were built.)

Telescopes

No one knows exactly when and where the telescope was first invented. The invention is usually attributed to a Dutch optician, Hans Lippershey (circa 1570-1619), in the autumn of 1608, although others claimed credit for the invention. Whatever the case, by early 1609 telescopes were on sale in Europe, and the Italian scientist Galileo Galilei heard of the invention, whereupon he built one of his own. Despite a popular misconception, Galileo himself did not invent the telescope.

Refractors and reflectors

All these early telescopes were of the so-called refracting type. Refracting telescopes use lenses to form and magnify an image. At the front of a refractor is the main light-collecting lens, called the *object glass*. This collects light and focuses it so it can be magnified by another lens, the *eyepiece*, at the other end of the tube. The larger the object glass the better, for the more light it can collect, the more clearly fainter objects can be seen and finer detail can be distinguished. A telescope's most vital statistic is the size of the *aperture* (the diameter of the object glass) rather than its power of magnification.

Early lenses were of poor quality. One of their faults was that they produced coloured fringes around images, because they spread out light like a prism. It was found that this problem could be avoided by using not a lens but a mirror to collect and focus light. The English scientist Sir Isaac Newton made the first reflecting telescope in 1668. In the Newtonian design, a concave (hollowed) mirror reflects light from the sky on to a smaller flat mirror or prism, which diverts the light to an eyepiece in the side of the tube. In the alternative

Refracting and reflecting telescopes. In a refractor (*top*) light is collected by a lens and focused into the eyepiece. In a reflector, the mirrors do the job.

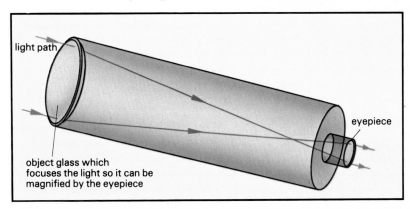

light path

eyepiece

object glass which focuses the light so it can be magnified by the eyepiece

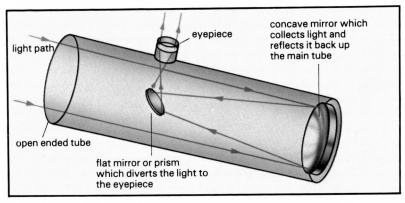

concave mirror which collects light and reflects it back up the main tube

eyepiece

light path

open ended tube

flat mirror or prism which diverts the light to the eyepiece

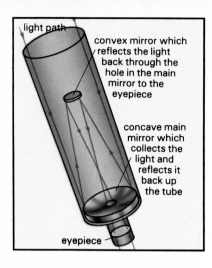

Above: A Cassegrain reflector, in which the eyepiece is set into a hole in the centre of the main mirror.

Cassegrain design, named after a French physicist, the light is reflected back through a hole in the centre of the main mirror. The secondary mirror in a reflector blocks some light from the main mirror, but otherwise

Left: Remains of Lord Rosse's giant reflector at Birr Castle, Ireland.

does not affect the image.

Reflectors have the advantage over refractors in that large mirrors can be made much more cheaply and easily than large lenses. Lenses have to be entirely transparent and can become distorted because they are supported only around the edges, whereas mirrors reflect light off their front surface and can be supported over their entire backs. The largest modern telescopes are all reflectors.

Astronomers were quick to experiment with the potential of reflectors. In the late 18th century, the English observer William Herschel began building giant reflecting telescopes with which he made many discoveries, including that of the planet Uranus in 1781, as well as many nebulae and star clusters. In 1783 he built a reflector with a mirror 46 centimetres (18 inches) in aperture, and in 1789 completed a reflector of 122 centimetres (48 inches) aperture, which was then the world's largest telescope. An even more impressive instrument was made in 1845 by the Earl of Rosse in Ireland. This gargantuan instrument had a mirror of 183 centimetres (72 inches) aperture with which Rosse discovered that many so-called nebulae were spiral in shape; this was the first step to establishing that these objects were actually galaxies, separate star 'cities' outside our own Milky Way.

All early reflectors had mirrors

made of a shiny metal called *speculum*, an alloy of copper and tin. This metal did not reflect light very efficiently and soon tarnished, so the mirror had to be repolished regularly. Because of these drawbacks, reflectors lost their popularity, particularly when the English optician John Dollond (1706-1761) showed in 1757 how to make refractors that produced colour-free images by combining lenses made of two sorts of glass. Such colour-free lenses are termed *achromatic*.

Giant telescopes

The world's greatest refracting telescopes were made by the company set up by the American optician Alvan Clark (1804-1877). Five times they set the record for the world's largest lens, beginning in 1862 with a 47-centimetre (18·5-inch) telescope with which the white-dwarf companion of Sirius was discovered, and culminating with instruments that remain the world's largest refractors: the 91-centimetre (36-inch) telescope at Lick Observatory, California, USA, built in 1888, and the 101-centimetre (40-inch) refractor of Yerkes Observatory, Wisconsin, USA, completed in 1897.

Since then, reflectors have regained popularity because of the introduction of glass mirrors coated with a

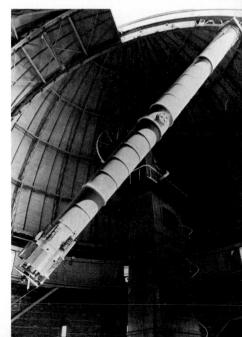

Right: The world's largest refractor, of 1-m (40 inches) aperture, at Yerkes Observatory.

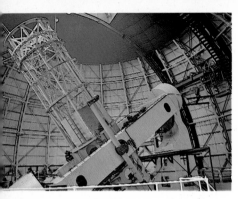

Above: The Mount Wilson 2·5-m reflector.

shiny layer of silver or aluminium. These reflect light much more efficiently than the old all-metal mirrors, and keep their shape without distorting. The first of the modern generation of giant glass mirrors was the 150-centimetre (60-inch) reflector on Mount Wilson, California, USA, set up by George Ellery Hale (1868-1938). Hale followed this in 1917 by installing on Mount Wilson the famous 250-centimetre (100-inch) reflector with which many important discoveries about the Universe have been made.

Below: The famous 5-m (200-inch) Hale reflector on Mount Palomar in California.

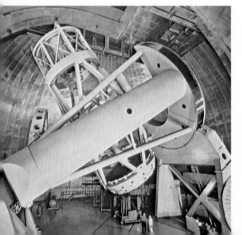

Below: Multiple-Mirror Telescope uses several smaller mirrors in place of one larger one.

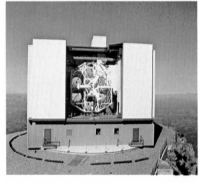

Still not satisfied, Hale determined to erect an even larger reflector, of 500 centimetres (200 inches) aperture. This was finally opened on Mount Palomar, California, USA, in 1948, after Hale's death; the telescope is known as the Hale Reflector in his honour. The 500-centimetre reflector remained the world's largest until 1976, when a 600-centimetre (236-inch) reflector was opened in the Soviet Union, in the Caucasus Mountains.

In 1979, a new design of reflector, called the Multiple Mirror Telescope, was opened on Mount Hopkins in Arizona, USA. This uses six mirrors each of 180 centimetres (72 inches) aperture to equal the performance of a single reflector 450 centimetres (176 inches) in diameter. More large optical telescopes may be built to this design in the future.

Schmidt telescopes

Conventional reflectors have tremendous light-gathering power, but their field of view is quite small. In 1930 an Estonian optician named Bernhard Schmidt (1879-1935) invented a telescope that combines lenses and mirrors to give a wide-angle view of the sky. The most famous of these Schmidt telescopes lies on Mount Palomar in California; it has

Right: Lenses and mirrors are used in the Schmidt telescope to collect and focus light.

a front lens of 122 centimetres (48 inches) aperture and a main mirror of 183 centimetres (72 inches) width. Schmidt telescopes are ideal for taking photographs of large areas of sky, particularly in search of faint objects such as comets and asteroids.

Below: Schmidt telescope on Mount Palomar takes wide-angle photographs of the sky.

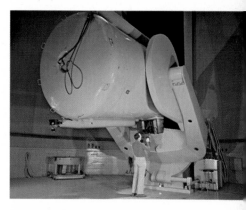

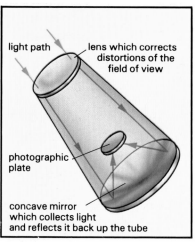

light path

lens which corrects distortions of the field of view

photographic plate

concave mirror which collects light and reflects it back up the tube

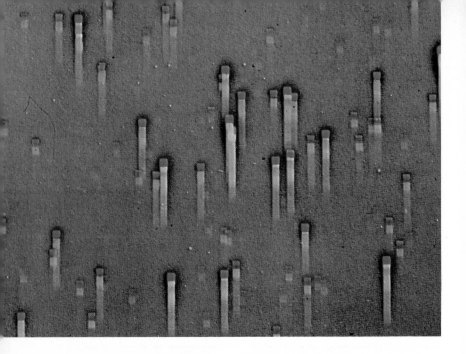

Colourful spectra of stars in the Hyades cluster, produced by a prism placed in front of the telescope eyepiece.

Analysing light and radio waves

Astronomers today seldom look directly through telescopes. Instead, they attach other instruments to record and analyse light from stars and galaxies. Often, the telescope is used like a giant telephoto lens to take pictures of celestial objects. A long-exposure photograph, which may be taken over several hours, reveals details, particularly in diffuse objects such as nebulae and galaxies, too faint to be seen by the eye.

The spectroscope

The main instrument astronomers use to analyse light is the spectroscope. This consists of a prism or grating that splits up light into its rainbow spectrum of colours. Specific dark or bright lines in the spectrum of an object reveal its composition. By using a spectroscope, astronomers can tell the gases of which stars, nebulae and the atmospheres of planets are made. It may seem like magic to analyse the composition of objects far off in space, but starlight contains much information which can be decoded by experts.

Radio telescopes

In recent years, astronomers have

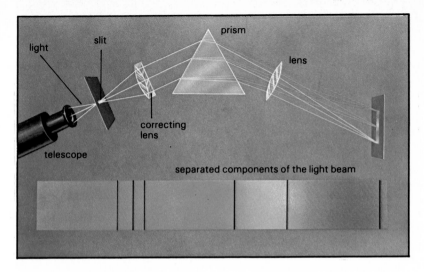

Above: A spectroscope splits up light into its constituent colours, revealing dark absorption bands, or Fraunhofer lines.

been able to study the sky at wavelengths other than those of visible light. After 1945, astronomers began to tune in to the Universe at radio wavelengths. Radio waves are of a similar nature to light, except that they are longer in wavelength. Our eyes are not sensitive to radio waves, but they can be detected by electronic equipment attached to radio telescopes. Most radio telescopes use large dish-shaped reflectors which collect radio waves and focus them on to a radio receiver. The waves are then amplified and recorded on magnetic tape.

Because radio waves are much longer than light waves, radio telescopes have to be much larger than optical telescopes to see the sky in as much detail. A famous radio telescope is that at Jodrell Bank in England, which has a dish 76 metres (250 feet) in diameter. It was the world's largest fully steerable radio telescope until the opening of a 100-metre

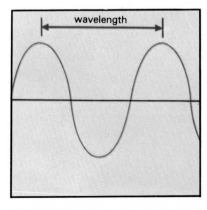

Right: Distance between two crests (or troughs) of radiation is its wavelength.

43

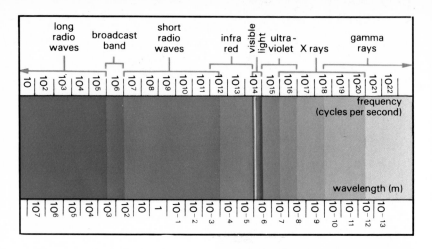

	long radio waves		broadcast band		short radio waves				infra red		visible light	ultra-violet	X rays		gamma rays		

frequency (cycles per second)

10 10^2 10^3 10^4 10^5 10^6 10^7 10^8 10^9 10^{10} 10^{11} 10^{12} 10^{13} 10^{14} 10^{15} 10^{16} 10^{17} 10^{18} 10^{19} 10^{20} 10^{21} 10^{22}

wavelength (m)

10^7 10^6 10^5 10^4 10^3 10^2 10 1 10^{-1} 10^{-2} 10^{-3} 10^{-4} 10^{-5} 10^{-6} 10^{-7} 10^{-8} 10^{-9} 10^{-10} 10^{-11} 10^{-12} 10^{-13}

Above: The electromagnetic spectrum, showing different regions.
Right: Effelsberg radio telescope in West Germany has a dish 100 m in diameter.

(328-foot) dish at the Effelsberg Observatory, West Germany, in 1971. The largest single radio astronomy dish of all is at Arecibo, Puerto Rico and is 305 metres (1000 feet) in diameter. It is so large it cannot be steered at all, but hangs like a circular hammock in a hollow between hills.

Sometimes, the output from several smaller radio telescopes is combined to produce the view of the sky that would be seen by one very large dish. This technique, called *aperture synthesis*, was originated at Cambridge, England, by a team under Sir Martin Ryle (born 1918). The main telescope at Cambridge has eight dishes of 12·8-metre (42-foot) dia-

Right: World's largest radio dish is 305 m in diameter, at Arecibo in Puerto Rico.

44

Above, left: Interlinked line of radio dishes 5 km long at Cambridge, England.

Above, right: Infrared Astronomical Satellite will map the sky at infrared wavelengths in 1982-83.

meter arranged in a line 5 kilometres (3 miles) long. By observing the sky over a period of time, this telescope produces the view that would be seen by a single radio dish 5 kilometres across (which would be impossible to build and steer on Earth, although such structures could eventually be built in the weightlessness of space). The largest aperture synthesis telescope of all is the Very Large Array in New Mexico, USA, which consists of 27 dishes, each of 25-metre (82-foot) diameter, arranged in a Y-shape pattern with arms up to 21 kilometres (13 miles) long. The Very Large Array equals the performance of a single dish 27 kilometres (17 miles) in diameter.

The future

Radio telescopes have made many important new discoveries about stars, galaxies and the Universe. Other exciting new discoveries are being made by space satellites which can detect radiation coming at wavelengths that are blocked by the Earth's atmosphere from reaching the ground. These wavelengths go by names such as infra-red, ultra-violet, X-rays, and gamma rays. During the 1980s, astronomers hope that the Space Telescope, a 240-centimetre (94-inch) reflecting telescope, will be placed in orbit. Above the blurring effect of the Earth's atmosphere, it will be possible to see the Universe in far more detail than ever before. Space is now producing a revolution in astronomy almost as great as that which followed the invention of the telescope over 350 years ago.

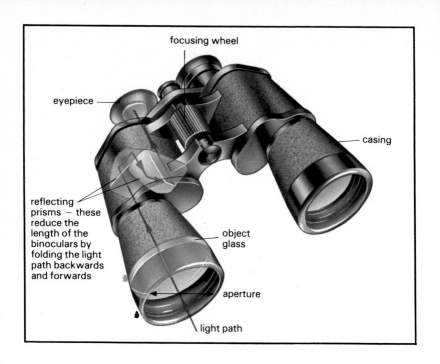

focusing wheel

eyepiece

casing

reflecting prisms — these reduce the length of the binoculars by folding the light path backwards and forwards

object glass

aperture

light path

Amateur observation

Binoculars are like two small refractors combined. Prisms inside the binoculars fold the light path to keep the instrument as compact as possible.

Binoculars

For those beginning astronomical observation, a pair of good binoculars is the ideal instrument. Binoculars are good value, and have the added advantage that they can be used for many purposes other than astronomy, and will still be needed even if you subsequently progress to a larger instrument.

Binoculars are given descriptions such as 8×30, 8×40, 7×50, or 10×50. The first number in the description indicates the magnification of the binoculars, while the second number gives the aperture of the object glass in millimetres. Most binoculars have apertures in the range from 30 to 50 millimetres (1·2 to 2 inches); larger binoculars are available, but are heavy and expensive. A magnification of 7 to 10 times is good for astronomical observing; it is tempting to go for the highest magnification possible, but remember that all the minor tremors in your hand will also be magnified by the same amount, and so it may prove impossible to keep the binoculars steady enough to see anything without using a tripod. Avoid cheap, very high-power binoculars, which are invariably of poor optical quality.

Binoculars are ideal for sky-sweeping, particularly across Milky Way star fields and in search of faint, fuzzy objects such as star clusters, nebulae, galaxies and comets. The constellation descriptions between pages 102 and 155 mention many objects suitable for observation through binoculars.

Telescopes

Small telescopes are usually much more expensive than binoculars. The term 'small' telescope refers to instruments with apertures of 50 to 60 millimetres (2 to 2·4 inches), which may magnify up to 100 times or more depending on the eyepiece being used (sets of interchangeable eye-pieces are used with astronomical telescopes). Telescopes of this size are all refractors. High magnifications (more than about 100 times) are useless on small telescopes, because the image becomes too distorted to see. A maximum magnification of 20 times for each 10 millimetres (50 for each inch) of aperture is a good 'rule of thumb'.

The increased light-gathering power and higher magnification of telescopes over binoculars will allow you to see finer detail on the Moon and planets and to resolve (distinguish between) double stars that

A simple refractor on a stand which allows the telescope to pivot up and down (in altitude) and around (in azimuth). Such a mounting is termed *altazimuth*.

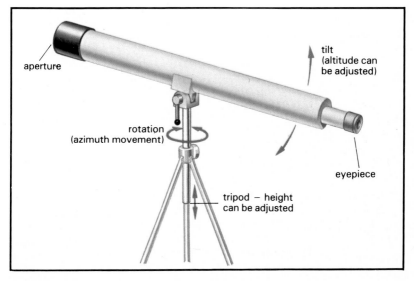

aperture

tilt
(altitude can
be adjusted)

rotation
(azimuth movement)

eyepiece

tripod – height
can be adjusted

are close together. But, for diffuse objects like nebulae, binoculars may still be better because their lower magnification and wider field of view increases the contrast of these fuzzy objects against the sky background. Some small telescopes (particularly the cheapest ones) can have very poor optics and be supported on wobbly mounts that are impossible to keep steady. These are a waste of money, and you would be better off with binoculars.

Telescopes of real value to the astronomer begin at apertures of 75 millimetres (3 inches), which are usually refractors, and 100 millimetres (4 inches), which can be refractors or reflectors. Alas, prices of telescopes in this size range start to increase literally astronomically. Perhaps the most popular instruments for serious amateur observing

are 150-millimetre and 220-millimetre (6-inch and 8·5-inch) reflectors. These bring most of the showpieces of the sky within reach, and they usually have mounts with motor drives that counteract the rotation of the Earth, to keep the telescope pointed at the object of interest. There will probably be a finder scope mounted on top. This is a small, low-powered telescope which is used to sight the main telescope.

Astrophotography

Even a camera can be used as an astronomical instrument. Any camera capable of taking a simple time exposure photograph can be left pointed at the sky with its shutter open for, say, 10 to 20 minutes. The film should show trails of stars, formed as the Earth rotated during the exposure. If you use a colour film, you can see the different colours of the stars. You may even catch sight of a meteor if you make the exposure at the time of a bright meteor shower such as the Perseids in August. Advanced astrophotographers guide their cameras to compensate for the Earth's rotation, or attach the camera body to the telescope in place of an eyepiece, using the telescope's optics as the camera lens. But in any case you will probably need to process your own films and prints to get the best results from your astrophotographs.

Left: Typical refracting telescope used by amateurs is mounted on a wooden tripod.

Above: Camera body attached to an amateur telescope for taking astrophotographs.

Below: Star trails, taken with a time exposure by a stationary camera.

The celestial sphere

Look up at the sky on a clear night. The sky seems to arch overhead like a vast star-studded dome. Ancient peoples believed that the stars were actually stuck on the inside of a sphere surrounding the Earth. Each day, the Sun and stars seem to move across the sky, rising in the east and setting in the west. The ancients attributed this motion to the rotation of the celestial sphere around the Earth.

Earth on the move

The apparent rotation of the celestial sphere means that the sky changes in appearance continually during each night. The night sky also looks different from season to season, and according to the latitude (angular distance north or south of the Equator) of your position. To many people today, the continually varying appearance of the sky is as baffling as it must have been to ancient man. Therefore, let's begin by trying to understand why the sky looks the way it does.

Firstly, of course, the Sun and stars do not really move of their own

Changing appearance of the sky in winter (*below left*) and summer, caused by the Earth's yearly motion around the Sun.

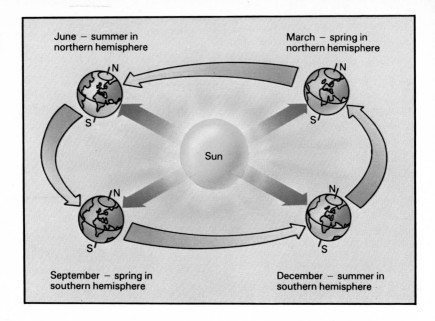

June — summer in
northern hemisphere

March — spring in
northern hemisphere

N

S

N

S

Sun

N

S

N

S

September — spring in
southern hemisphere

December — summer in
southern hemisphere

accord around the heavens each day; it is actually the daily rotation of the Earth on its axis that makes them appear to move so (although astronomers still find it convenient to retain the concept of the celestial sphere for some purposes, such as measuring celestial coordinates).

Since the Earth takes 24 hours to rotate through 360°, then for each hour of time the stars will appear to move 15° across the sky. The Earth's daily rotation, obtained from the observation of stars, is the basis of our timekeeping, which is why time services are based at the world's major observatories, for example the Royal Greenwich Observatory in England and the US Naval Observatory in Washington, DC.

Seasons are caused as the Earth orbits the Sun. First one Pole and then the other tilts towards the Sun.

But the Earth does not only spin on its axis. It is also moving on its orbit around the Sun. The time taken for the Earth to orbit the Sun once is known as a year; it lasts approximately 365 days 6 hours. Our calendar year of 365 days is based on the Earth's orbital motion around the Sun. Because the Earth does not orbit the Sun in an exact number of days, we have to add an extra day to the calendar every four years to keep the calendar in step with the seasons. Each year containing an extra day is called a leap year.

As a result of the Earth's orbital motion, the Sun appears to change

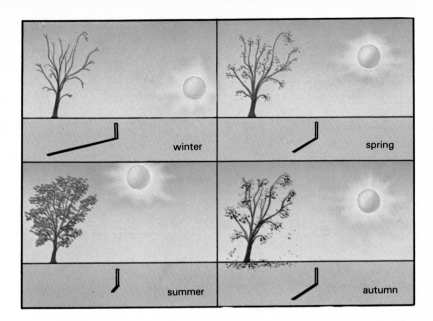

winter	spring
summer	autumn

Different altitudes of the Sun from season to season can be measured by the length of shadows it casts.

position slightly (approximately one degree) against the star background from day to day. Therefore, the stars appear to rise about four minutes earlier each night.

An additional confusion is that the Earth's axis of rotation is not perpendicular (at right angles) to the plane of its orbit, but instead tilts at an angle of 23·5° from the vertical. This tilt of the Earth's axis causes the seasons. In June, the Earth's North Pole is tilted 23·5° towards the Sun and so there is summer in the northern hemisphere. Six months later, in December, the South Pole is presented to the Sun, causing summer in the southern hemisphere. Therefore, during the year, the Sun seems to stray from a maximum of 23·5° north of the Equator to 23·5° south of the Equator. The Sun's apparent yearly path around the sky against the star background (which, remember, is caused entirely by the Earth's orbital motion and axial tilt) is termed the *ecliptic.*

You can, if you wish, follow the Sun's yearly motion around the sky by placing a stick firmly in the ground. In the summer, at noon, the stick's shadow cast by the Sun will be shortest, whereas in the winter when the Sun is lowest in the sky, the shadow will be at its longest.

In summer, the days last longer than the nights, while the opposite is true in winter. But on two days each year, night and day are equal in length. These are the occasions on which the Sun crosses the celestial equator, and are known as the *equinoxes* (a name which means equal night). The vernal, or spring, equinox occurs on 21 March; the autumnal equinox is on 23 September. (In some years, these dates may slip by one day – but the insertion of an extra day in the calendar every fourth year brings them back on schedule!)

There is one more effect we need to take into account to complete our understanding of the appearance of the sky, and that is the effect of

Visibility of stars depends on their position on the celestial sphere, and the observer's latitude.

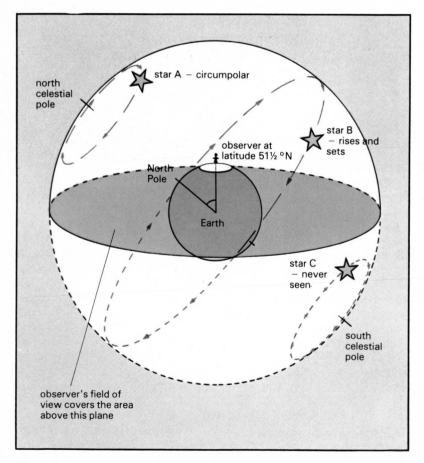

north celestial pole

star A – circumpolar

star B – rises and sets

observer at latitude 51½ °N

North Pole

Earth

star C – never seen

south celestial pole

observer's field of view covers the area above this plane

changes in latitude. An observer at one of the Earth's poles would see only half the sky. Above would lie the celestial pole; the celestial equator would be just on the horizon. Each night, the stars would spin around the pole, with none appearing to rise or set. An observer standing at the Earth's Equator, by contrast, would see the celestial poles lying on the north and south horizon respectively, and the celestial equator would be above. Each night, stars would appear to rise in the east, move overhead, and set in the west as the Earth turned. During one year, an observer at the Equator would see the entire sky.

Observers stationed at latitudes on Earth midway between the poles and the Equator see an intermediate amount of the sky. Some stars appear to circle the pole each night without setting (these are called *circumpolar stars*) while others rise and set. The angle of the celestial pole above the horizon shows your latitude on Earth. For example, at latitude 55° north, the north celestial pole will be 55° above the horizon. Inhabitants of the Earth's northern hemisphere can easily check their latitude, because a fairly bright star, Polaris, lies close to the north celestial pole. Unfortunately, there is no equivalent star near the south celestial pole.

Astronomical coordinates

Astronomers use a system of coordin-

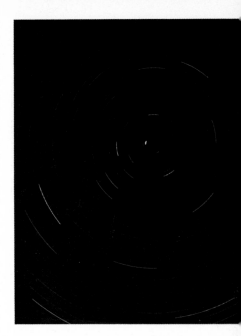

Star trails around the north celestial pole photographed in a time exposure by a stationary camera. The bright star near the centre is Polaris.

ates for measuring star positions that is similar to the system of longitude and latitude used on Earth, except that in the sky the coordinates are termed *right ascension* and *declination* respectively. Right ascension is measured from the vernal equinox (one of the two points where the celestial equator and the ecliptic intersect) which is the equivalent of the Greenwich Meridian (0° longitude) on Earth. Right ascension is calibrated in hours, minutes and seconds because of the relationship between the rotation of the Earth and time.

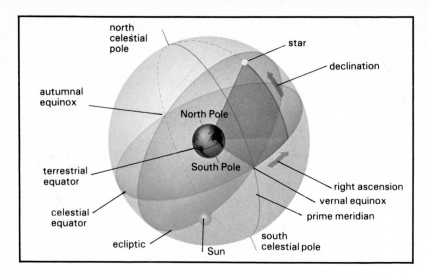

Above: Coordinates on the celestial sphere.

Below: Precession occurs as the Earth wobbles slowly in space like a spinning top every 26 000 years.

Declination is measured like terrestrial latitude in degrees of arc (°) north or south of the celestial equator. Declination north of the celestial equator is indicated by +, to the south it is indicated by −.

All this would be straightforward, were it not for the fact that the Earth wobbles slowly in space like a spinning top. This wobble is termed *precession*. Because of precession, the Earth's axis traces out a circle on the celestial sphere every 26 000 years (a cycle of precession). Therefore the positions of the celestial poles move imperceptibly all the time against the star background – and so do the two equinoxes. This means that a star's celestial coordinates change slowly with time. At present, the vernal equinox (the zero point of right ascension) lies in the constellation Pisces, although about 2000 years ago

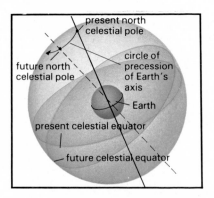

it lay in Aries. It will next move on into Aquarius, but will not reach there for 600 years yet – so the much-heralded age of Aquarius is still a long way off!

Looking at galaxies

Our Sun is one of at least 100 000 million stars that make up the pinwheel-shaped system known as the Galaxy. As we saw on page 30, the American astronomer Harlow Shapley in 1918 established that the Sun lies in the suburbs of our Galaxy. The stars which make up the constellations are relatively near to us in the Galaxy. The more distant members of the Galaxy crowd together in the faint hazy band popularly called the Milky Way. (The word 'galaxy' comes from the Greek 'galactos', meaning milk.) When we look at the Milky Way we are seeing the rim of our Galaxy from the inside, and the term Milky Way is often used when referring to our entire Galaxy. Most of the stars are in one plane, interspersed with lanes of dark dust which obscure light from the stars behind. This flat plane of stars is arranged around a bulging core, which, as seen from Earth, lies in the direction of the constellation Sagittarius.

But what would the Galaxy look like if seen from above, in plan view? Astronomers have been able to survey the overall shape of our Galaxy by plotting the distribution of bright stars and clusters, and also by detecting the radio emission given off by

Sun's position in the Galaxy, two-thirds of the way from the centre out to the rim.

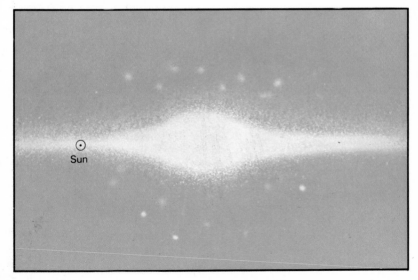

Sun

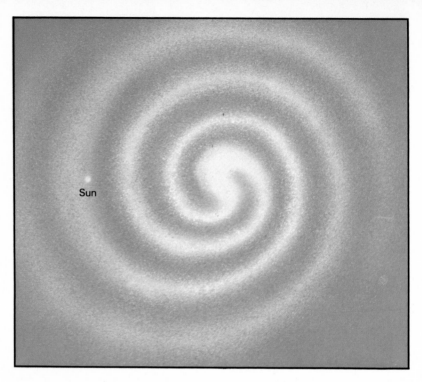

Plan view of our Galaxy, showing spiral arms that astronomers believe exist.

hydrogen gas between the stars. Our Milky Way Galaxy turns out to be spiral in shape, with the Sun lying on the inner edge of one of the spiral arms. This particular arm also contains the star-formation region of the constellation Orion and the North American Nebula in Cygnus. The dense star fields of Sagittarius lie in an arm closer to the Galaxy's centre.

Classifying galaxies

How typical of galaxies is our Milky Way? After the American astro-nomer Edwin Hubble had establish-ed in the 1920s that other galaxies exist outside our own, he went on to classify them according to their shape: spirals, barred spirals, elliptic-als and irregulars. Spiral galaxies are designated by a capital S; they are further sub-divided into types a, b, and c depending on how tightly the arms are wound, with Sa spirals being the tightest and Sc the loosest. Barred spirals (galaxies with a bar of stars across the centre, from the ends of which the spiral arms emerge) are designated SB, followed by lower-case letters to indicate the tightness and complexity of the arms. Elliptical galaxies range from E0, which are perfectly spherical, to E7, which are lens-shaped and are one stage away from the S0 type which possesses a disc but only embryo spiral arms. Our own Galaxy is believed to be an average spiral (Sb type on Hubble's classification). From afar, our Milky Way Galaxy would look like the Andromeda spiral, or perhaps like M101 in Ursa Major.

Spiral galaxies have a dense core of old stars, while their outer spiral

Classification of galaxies devised by Edwin Hubble, with examples of each type.

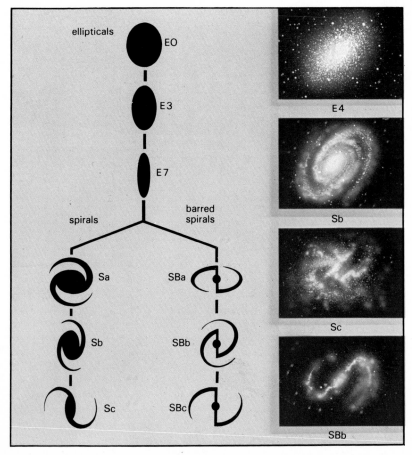

regions contain younger stars plus much dust and gas, like the Orion Nebula, which still has to form into stars. Elliptical galaxies, on the other hand, contain mainly old stars, and almost no dust or gas. For them, star formation has finished.

Astronomers once assumed that galaxies evolved from one type into another as they aged, but they now believe that all the galaxies were formed at the same time and remain the same type throughout their lives. Whether a galaxy becomes a spiral or an elliptical probably depends on how quickly the gas cloud was spinning that gave birth to the galaxy, with spiral galaxies being the fastest spinners and ellipticals the slowest.

Spiral galaxies range from about 20 000 to 100 000 light years or more in diameter, and contain from 1000 million to over 100 000 million stars. So our own Milky Way is among the largest of spirals. Over half the galaxies visible are ordinary spirals; another quarter of all galaxies are barred spirals. Most of the remaining galaxies are ellipticals, which fall into two classes: giants and dwarfs. Giant ellipticals, which are rare, include the biggest and brightest galaxies in the Universe. They can be up to several hundred thousand light years across, and contain the mass of 10 million million stars.

By contrast, dwarf ellipticals are the smallest galaxies known, measuring only about 5000 light years across and containing a few million stars. Two small elliptical galaxies accom-

Right: Barred spiral galaxy NGC 3992 in Ursa Major has a bright core and a short bar. Its spiral arms form a ring, giving it the shape of the Greek letter Theta.

pany the Andromeda spiral, M 31 (see page 33), and are visible in amateur instruments. Dwarf ellipticals may be the most abundant type of galaxy (they are certainly the majority in our Local Group) but they are so small and faint that it is difficult to spot any except the nearest. Irregular galaxies, which have no distinct shape at all, make up a small percentage of known galaxies. The so-called Magellanic Clouds which accompany our Milky Way are small irregular galaxies.

Naming galaxies

There are two systems of nomenclature commonly used by astronomers, that of Messier's catalogue of celestial objects of hazy and distended appearance; and that of the New General Catalogue of nebulae and other celestial objects of distended appearance. Objects listed in the first catalogue are given the letter M followed by a number; those in the second catalogue are given the letters NGC followed by a number. Since one object may be listed in both catalogues it will therefore have M and NGC designations which may be used as alternatives. For example, the Andromeda Galaxy, M 31, is also known as NGC 224.

Right: Giant elliptical galaxy M 87 in Virgo is surrounded by a swarm of globular star clusters.

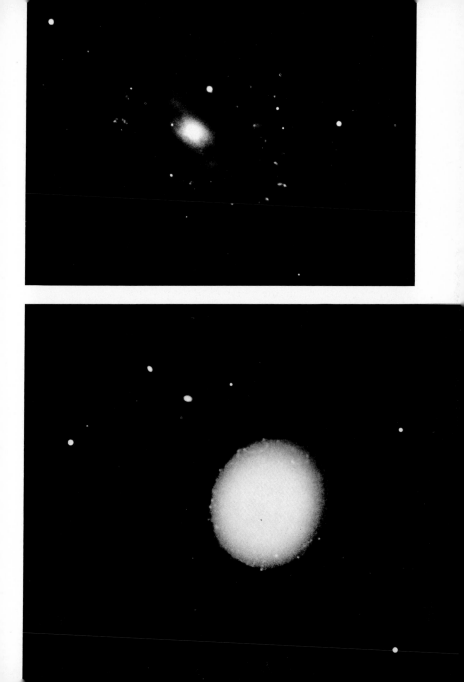

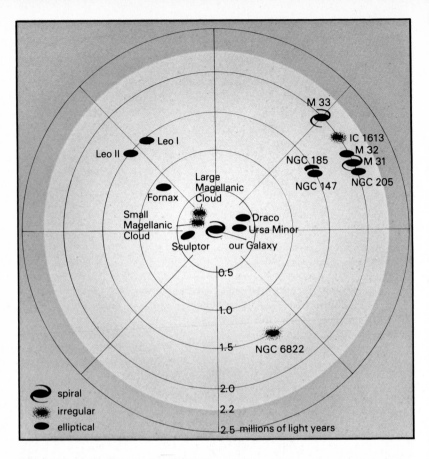

M 33

IC 1613
M 32
M 31
NGC 185
NGC 205
NGC 147

Leo I
Leo II

Large
Magellanic
Cloud

Fornax

Small
Magellanic
Cloud

Draco
Ursa Minor

Sculptor   our Galaxy

0.5

1.0

1.5   NGC 6822

2.0

2.2

spiral

irregular

elliptical

2.5 millions of light years

The Local Group

Galaxies seem to gather together in clusters of various sizes. Our own Milky Way Galaxy is a member of a small cluster of about 30 known galaxies, called the Local Group. The Andromeda Galaxy and the Milky Way are the largest members. Third largest is the spiral galaxy

M 33 in Triangulum, which is just visible through amateur instruments. The other members of the Local Group are all very faint, such as the Magellanic Clouds and the satellites of the Andromeda Galaxy. Some of them are visible only on long-exposure photographs taken through large telescopes.

A large and famous cluster, containing many thousands of galaxies of all shapes and sizes, is the Virgo Cluster, about 40 million light years away. The brightest members of this cluster can be detected through amateur telescopes. The cluster lies in the constellation Virgo, and overlaps into neighbouring Coma Berenices.

Observing galaxies

Galaxies, being diffuse and faint, require similar observation techniques to nebulae: telescopes with low powers of magnification and a wide field of view to increase contrast. This is particularly important when trying to locate galaxies, since they may be invisible through the telescope's finder and you will have to sweep over a wide area of sky for them.

Through the telescope, a galaxy looks like a rounded or elongated fuzzy patch, depending on the type of galaxy and the angle at which it is presented to us. Many galaxies show a star-like central nucleus, but you will need quite a large telescope to detect the spiral arms and dust lanes in even the brightest galaxies.

Before looking for faint objects such as galaxies and nebulae you will need to wait at least 10 minutes for your eyes to become properly adapted to the dark. One useful trick when studying faint objects is to look not directly at them, but to turn your gaze very slightly to one side, so that light from the object falls on the more sensitive outer regions of your eye. This technique is known as *averted vision.*

Cluster of galaxies in Virgo, about 40 million light years away. Three thousand galaxies have been found in this cluster.

Peculiar galaxies

Some galaxies have particular characteristics that make them different from the more usual galaxies like our own. For example, certain galaxies seem to be suffering some kind of explosion, as is apparently the case with M 82 in Ursa Major. M 82, in common with other peculiar-looking galaxies, is a source of radio noise. Such objects are called *radio galaxies*. Famous examples of radio galaxies visible in modest amateur telescopes

are the giant elliptical galaxy M 87 in Virgo and NGC 5128 in Centaurus. Both these galaxies seem to be sites of multiple explosions.

As astronomers have probed ever deeper into space, they have come across increasing numbers of unusual galaxies. Prominent among these are the so-called *Seyfert galaxies*, named after the American astronomer Carl Seyfert (1911-1960) who drew attention to them in 1943. These are spiral

Peculiar galaxy M82 in Ursa Major is a source of radio noise.

Above: Peculiar galaxy NGC 5128 is also known as the radio source Centaurus A.

Above: Seyfert galaxy NGC 1275, known as Perseus A, is a source of radio noise.

galaxies with very brilliant central cores. Even more bizarre are the objects known as *quasars*, which at first glance look like faint stars but which are actually believed to be far-off galaxies in the process of formation.

This view is supported by the fact that many quasars are surrounded by faint fuzzy haloes like the outer regions of a galaxy. Quasars therefore seem to be more extreme versions of radio galaxies and Seyfert galaxies.

Quasars shine as brightly as thousands of normal galaxies like the Milky Way, which is why we can see them over such vast distances – even the nearest are several thousand million light years away, and the farthest are believed to be the most remote objects visible. One popular theory is that quasars and their relatives get their energy from massive black holes (see page 89) at their centres, which tear apart stars and suck in the gas. Perhaps, as the black holes eat up all the gas, the brilliance of the cores dies away and the objects fade until they resemble normal galaxies.

Looking at stars

Dense Milky Way star fields towards the
centre of the Galaxy in Sagittarius.

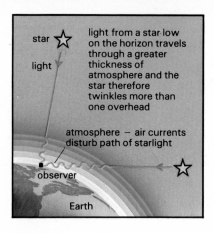

Light from stars is distorted by the atmosphere, causing twinkling.

At first, the number of stars on a clear, dark night seems countless. In fact, no more than about 1500 stars are visible to the naked eye at any one time, even under the best conditions. All these stars are relatively close neighbours of the Sun – within a few thousand light years. Many stars (particularly the bright ones) seem to twinkle. This is nothing to do with the stars themselves, but is an effect of the Earth's atmosphere. Air currents make starlight dance around as it passes through our atmosphere, thereby causing the twinkling effect. Stars near the horizon twinkle the most, for we are looking at them through a denser layer of atmosphere. Such stars often appear to flash different colours, from red to blue. This is caused by the atmosphere breaking up the starlight like a prism. The amount of twinkling on a given night shows how unsteady the atmosphere is.

The steadiness of the atmosphere affects the viewing conditions through a telescope. Turbulent air produces an effect like heat haze when seen through a telescope, blurring the image. This is termed 'bad seeing'. To get the best performance from your telescope, for example for distinguishing close double stars or detecting fine detail on the Moon and planets, you must wait for a night of 'good seeing'.

The constellations

Many of the brightest stars in our Galaxy form distinctive patterns. Early peoples visualized these sky patterns as representing their gods and heroes, and named the star groups accordingly. Thus the first constellations were introduced. Modern astronomers retain these constellations as a convenient way of dividing up the sky. A total of 88 constellations now fills the entire sky, but some of these are of relatively recent origin.

Around 150 AD the Greek astronomer Ptolemy listed 48 constellations in his book the Almagest. Several of these, particularly the 12 constellations of the Zodiac (see glossary), are believed to have originated from Middle Eastern populations at the dawn of civilization thousands of years ago, although others were of Greek invention. Various additions have since been made

to Ptolemy's classical list of ancient constellations. In 1603 the German astronomer Johann Bayer (1572-1625) published a star atlas called 'Uranometria', in which he introduced 12 new constellations of the southern sky: Apus, Chamaeleon, Dorado, Grus, Hydrus, Indus, Musca, Pavo, Phoenix, Triangulum Australe, Tucana, and Volans.

Another seven constellations now accepted by astronomers were introduced by the Polish observer Johannes Hevelius (1611-1687) on star maps published posthumously in 1690. These constellations are Canes Venatici, Lacerta, Leo Minor, Lynx,

Star map of constellations visible from the northern hemisphere, drawn up by the Polish astronomer Johannes Hevelius.

Scutum, Sextans, and Vulpecula. Fourteen more constellations, all in the southern skies, we owe to the French astronomer Nicolas Louis de Lacaille (1713-1762), who made extensive observations of the southern skies from the Cape of Good Hope in 1751 to 1753. Lacaille's constellations (many of them unfortunately faint and uninteresting) are: Antlia, Caelum, Circinus, Fornax, Horologium, Mensa, Microscopium, Norma, Octans, Pictor, Pyxis, Reticulum, Sculptor, and Telescopium.

NICOLAS - LOUIS
LA CAILLE
ASTRONOME
1713 — 1762

Other constellations have been suggested by various astronomers in the past, but most of these groupings are not used now. In 1930 the International Astronomical Union drew up the modern list, which all astronomers now use, of constellations and their boundaries.

Naming stars

Stars are given various different names and designations. Many of the

Monument to Nicolas Louis de Lacaille, who mapped the southern skies from the Cape of Good Hope.

star names we use are of Arabic origin, such as Aldebaran, Betelgeuse and Rigel, although others, for example Sirius and Procyon, are Greek. Stars are also labelled with Greek letters such as Alpha. This lettering system was introduced by Johann Bayer in 1603, and has since been generally adopted. Stars which are assigned no Greek letter are known instead by a number and the name of the constellation, for example 61 Cygni. These numbers are called *Flamsteed numbers* because they were appended to the catalogue of stars compiled by the first English astronomer royal, John Flamsteed (1646-1719). Variable stars are usually given Roman letters; as R Andromedae. Still other catalogues give their own designations to stars, so that stellar nomenclature can be highly confusing. But the system of proper names, Bayer letters, and Flamsteed numbers is most commonly used for stars visible to the naked eye.

Star families

Telescopes show that many stars are not single stars but have companions. Such twin-star systems are known as *double stars*. In some cases the two stars lie in the same line of sight when viewed from Earth, but may actually be at vastly differing distances from us. These are *optical doubles*. The great majority of stellar twins are, however, physically related, orbiting each other over long periods of time, and are called *binary stars*. Famous examples within easy range of small telescopes, or even binoculars, are Beta

Above, right: When two unrelated stars lie by chance in the same line of sight, the observer sees a so-called optical double. *Right:* In a genuine binary, two stars orbit their common centre of gravity.

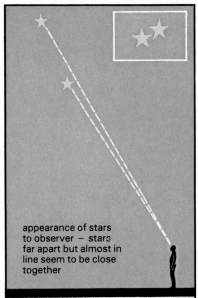

appearance of stars to observer — stars far apart but almost in line seem to be close together

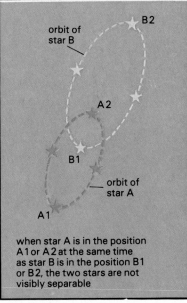

orbit of star B

B2

A2

B1

orbit of star A

A1

when star A is in the position A1 or A2 at the same time as star B is in the position B1 or B2, the two stars are not visibly separable

Cygni (also called Albireo), Gamma Leonis, Alpha Centauri and Alpha Crucis. In a binary star, the brighter star is known as the *primary*, while the fainter star is the *secondary*. The double nature of very close pairs of stars may only be revealed by analysis of their light in spectroscopes. These are *spectroscopic binaries*.

There are more complicated stellar families – triples, quadruples and even larger groups. The star Castor, in Gemini, is actually a system of six stars bound together by gravity, although not all of them can be seen separately through telescopes.

The Pleiades are a young cluster of bright blue stars in the constellation Taurus, still surrounded by wispy remnants of the cloud from which they formed.

Some stars gather together in clusters of dozens or even many thousands, all born about the same time in the same area of Space. A famous example is the Pleiades cluster in Taurus, of which six or seven members are visible to the naked eye, while telescopes reveal up to 200 members. Clusters like the Pleiades are of irregular shape, and contain young stars, formed relatively recently within the past few million years. But distributed around our Galaxy are much larger, globular-shaped clusters of very old stars. These *globular clusters*, of which about 125 are known, contain a quarter of a million stars or more. They are believed to have formed early in the history of our Galaxy, at least 10 000 million

Globular star cluster M 15 in Pegasus, easily visible through binoculars. It lies about 35 000 light years away. M 15 has been found to be an X-ray source.

years ago, and contain some of the oldest stars known. Examples are M 13 in Hercules, and Omega Centauri and 47 Tucanae in the southern skies. Many more examples of double and multiple stars and star clusters for you to observe are given in the constellation descriptions.

Star brightnesses

The brightness of a star is termed its magnitude. The magnitude system began about 130 BC with the Greek astronomer Hipparchus who divided

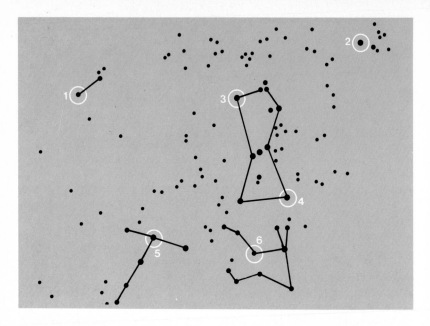

stars into six magnitude classes from the brightest of all (first magnitude) to the faintest visible to the naked eye (sixth magnitude). Since then, this scale has been put on a more scientific footing, so that a sixth-magnitude star is now defined as being exactly 100 times fainter than a first-magnitude star. Each magnitude step thus corresponds to a brightness difference of approximately 2·5 times. An object's *apparent magnitude* (or mag) is how bright it appears to us in the sky. Its *absolute magnitude* is the brightness it would have if it were at a standard distance of 32·6 light years.

But some stars are more than 100 times brighter than sixth-magnitude stars. These are given negative magnitudes, such as Arcturus, of magni-

tude −0·06, and Sirius, the brightest star in the sky, which is of magnitude −1·5. On this scale, the planet Venus at its brightest is of magnitude −4·4, and the Sun is of magnitude −26·8. At the other end of the scale, stars fainter than sixth magnitude are given increasingly large positive magnitudes. For instance, a telescope of 60 millimetres aperture has a range down to about magnitude 10, while the faintest stars ever detected by telescopes on Earth are approximately magnitude 24. The magnitude system may seem cumbersome and confusing, but it does have the merit that it can be extended indefinitely in either direction.

Varying stars

Closer inspection of the sky shows that not all stars are constant in brightness. Some of them seem to vary in intensity over periods of days or even months. Occasionally, bright new stars pop up where no star was seen before. A catalogue published in 1975 listed over 25 000 variable stars, and more are being discovered all the time. Amateur observers can follow the brightness changes of variable stars by comparing them with nearby stars of known constant brightness. Often, these observations can be of real value to professional astronomers who are too busy to keep their own check on all variable stars.

There are several reasons why stars vary in brightness. One reason is that the star is unstable in size, as are the highly bloated giant and supergiant red stars. The first variable star to be discovered was a red giant called Mira, in the constellation Cetus. This star was first noted in 1596 by the Dutch astronomer David Fabricius (1564-1617), but it soon faded out of sight. Mira was next observed by Johann Bayer, who included it on his star atlas of 1603. Mira fluctuates between about second and 10th magnitude every 11 months. Another famous red star which varies in size and brightness is Betelgeuse in Orion, although its magnitude fluctuations are nothing like as startling as those of Mira. Betelgeuse varies irregularly between magnitude 0·4 and 1·3, changing from between 300 to 400 times the size of the Sun as it does so.

Light curve of the long-period red giant variable star Mira. Its brightness fluctuates between about second and tenth magnitude in an average of 331 days.

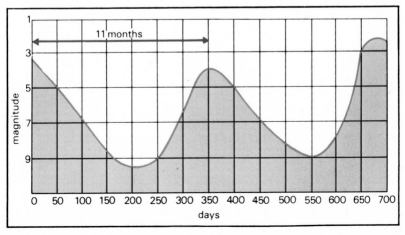

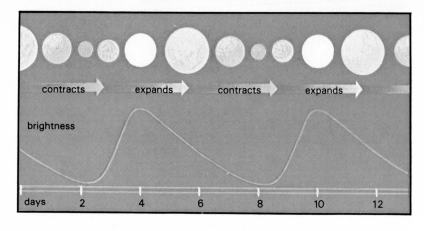

contracts ➡ expands ➡ contracts ➡ expands ➡

brightness

days 2 4 6 8 10 12

Cepheid variables An important class of variable star is that which pulsates regularly in size, like a beating heart. Such stars are known as Cepheid variables, after their prototype Delta Cephei, whose variability was discovered in 1784 by the deaf-mute English astronomer John Goodricke (1764-1786), who died at age 21. Delta Cephei oscillates in size every 5·4 days, changing in brightness from magnitude 3·6 to 4·3 as it does so. In 1912, the American astronomer Henrietta Leavitt (1868-1921) discovered that there is a relationship between the period of a Cepheid variable's light variations and the star's intrinsic brightness: the longer the star's cycle of variations, the brighter it is. Therefore one can work out the real brightness (the wattage) of a Cepheid by measuring its period. But the star's apparent brightness in the sky will be affected by its distance from us. So by comparing the calculated brightness of a

A Cepheid variable changes in brightness as it swells and contracts.

Cepheid with its observed brightness, astronomers can work out how far away it must be. Cepheid variables are therefore important as distance indicators (*standard candles*) in astronomy.

Eclipsing binaries Another common type of variable star, these are close double stars in which one star periodically passes in front of the other. Such a stellar eclipse temporarily reduces the total amount of light we receive from the system. The star thus appears to fluctuate regularly in brightness as seen from Earth, although the members of the binary are not intrinsically variable. The prototype eclipsing binary is Algol (Beta Persei), whose light fluctuations were observed and explained by John Goodricke in 1782.

Novae Some stars erupt suddenly in brightness. These are novae, a word

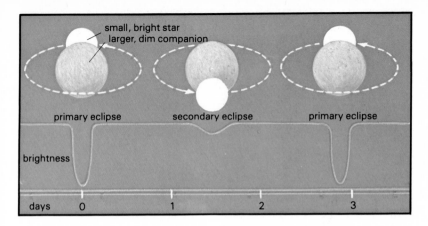

small, bright star
larger, dim companion

primary eclipse secondary eclipse primary eclipse

brightness

days 0 1 2 3

which means 'new', for they were once thought to be genuinely new stars. A nova appears temporarily where no star was seen before, and then fades out of view again, but it is not a new star. Instead, novae are thought to be close binary systems in which gas flows from one star to the other and ignites in a nuclear eruption, causing the sudden surge in

Above: In an eclipsing binary, the combined light output of the two stars changes as they pass each other.

brightness and throwing off a shell of gas. Several novae have erupted more than once; perhaps all novae suffer multiple outbursts given time.

Below: A nova is caused when gas flows from a star to a companion white dwarf and ignites in a nuclear eruption.

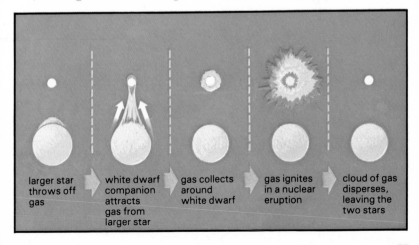

larger star throws off gas

white dwarf companion attracts gas from larger star

gas collects around white dwarf

gas ignites in a nuclear eruption

cloud of gas disperses, leaving the two stars

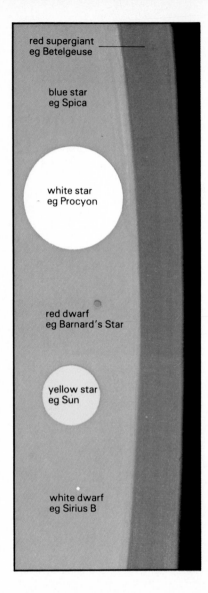

red supergiant
eg Betelgeuse

blue star
eg Spica

white star
eg Procyon

red dwarf
eg Barnard's Star

yellow star
eg Sun

white dwarf
eg Sirius B

Comparison of the sizes and colours of
stars, from dwarfs to supergiants.

Far more catastrophic explosions are
those of supernovae, in which entire
stars blow themselves to bits. No
supernova has been seen in our Galaxy since 1604, so we are long over-
due for another one (ordinary novae,
by contrast, are fairly common).
Supernovae are dealt with in more
detail later in this chapter.

Colours of stars
Although at first glance all stars appear white, more careful inspection
shows that some of them have distinct
colours. These colours are more prominent when viewed through binoculars. A star's colour tells us how hot
it is at the surface (inside, it is very
much hotter).

Red stars are the coolest; orange
and yellow stars are hotter; while
white and blue-white stars are the
hottest of all. The most prominent
colours are those of red giant and
supergiant stars, such as Aldebaran,
Antares and Betelgeuse. These stars
are swelling up in size at the ends of
their lives, as astronomers predict the
Sun will do eventually. Red giant
and supergiant stars are several tens
or even hundreds of times the size of
our Sun, which is why they are so
bright despite their low surface temperatures of about 3000°C. There
also exist red dwarf stars, which, as
their name implies, are small and
cool. Because of their small size even
the nearest of them is too faint to see
without a telescope.

Orange stars can also be giants or
dwarfs. An example of an orange

giant is Arcturus, while Epsilon Eridani is an orange dwarf. In each case, their surface temperature is about 4000°C. Yellow stars, such as the Sun and Capella, are considerably hotter, with temperatures of about 6000°C. Pure white stars, such as Canopus and Procyon, have surface temperatures of around 7500°C. Hotter stars, for example Sirius and Vega, with temperatures of around 10 000°C, appear blue-white. The hottest stars of all, with temperatures of 20 000°C or more, have a distinctly bluish tinge. Examples are Rigel and Spica.

The Orion Nebula, a star 'factory' within which new stars are forming even today.

Life of stars

Star birth

Stars are incandescent balls of gas, giving out their own heat and light, and similar to our own Sun. But how are stars born? What keeps them glowing? And how do they grow old and die? Astronomers believe they now have answers to most of these questions.

Stars are thought to be formed from giant clouds of dust and gas in space, known as *nebulae*. One famous site of star formation is the great nebula in Orion, visible to the naked eye as a hazy patch, and particularly

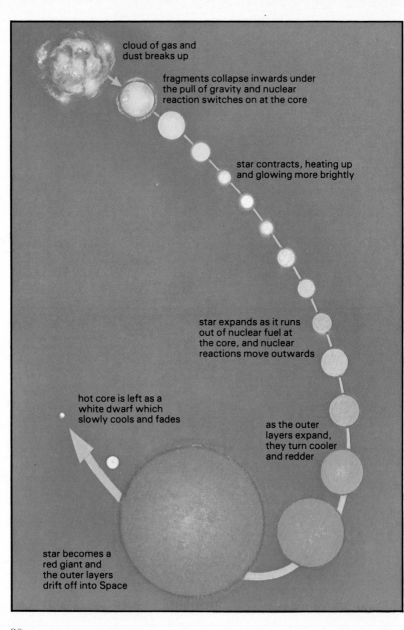

cloud of gas and dust breaks up

fragments collapse inwards under the pull of gravity and nuclear reaction switches on at the core

star contracts, heating up and glowing more brightly

star expands as it runs out of nuclear fuel at the core, and nuclear reactions move outwards

hot core is left as a white dwarf which slowly cools and fades

as the outer layers expand, they turn cooler and redder

star becomes a red giant and the outer layers drift off into Space

impressive viewed through binoculars or telescopes. Stars are forming today inside the Orion Nebula; several newborn stars are visible through small telescopes at the nebula's centre, making up the group known as the 'Trapezium'. Radiation from the largest and hottest of these stars makes the whole nebula glow.

Stars start to form when part of a gas cloud like the Orion Nebula breaks up into individual blobs as a result of random swirling motions in the cloud. These blobs collapse under the inward pull of their own gravity. As they shrink, becoming smaller and denser, pressures and temperatures build up inside them until nuclear reactions switch on at their cores. When that happens, a gas blob becomes a true star.

Stars, it seems, do not come into being on their own, but in vast groups. The Orion Nebula is estimated to contain enough material to form a whole cluster of stars. The Pleiades Cluster in Taurus is an example of a star group that has recently formed from a giant gas cloud. Long-exposure photographs show the stars of the Pleiades to be surrounded by wisps of dust and gas, remnants of the cloud which gave birth to them. Our Sun was probably a member of a similar cluster when it was born 4700 million years ago, but the stars of that cluster have long since drifted apart, as will eventually happen to the Pleiades.

Left: Life cycle of a star like the Sun.

Other famous areas of star formation visible to amateur astronomers include the Lagoon Nebula (M 8) in Sagittarius and the Tarantula Nebula in the Large Magellanic Cloud. Nebulae like these are best viewed through instruments with low magnification and a wide field of view, to increase their contrast against the sky background. Binoculars can therefore be as good as telescopes in locating such diffuse objects. You should wait for dark, clear nights to observe nebulae, for even the slightest haze can drown them from sight.

Some nebulae contain no illuminating stars, and are therefore dark. These can only be seen in silhouette against a brighter background such as another bright nebula or the Milky Way star field. The most famous example of a dark nebula is the Coalsack in the constellation of the Southern Cross.

The Coalsack Nebula, a dark cloud of dust seen silhouetted against the Milky Way.

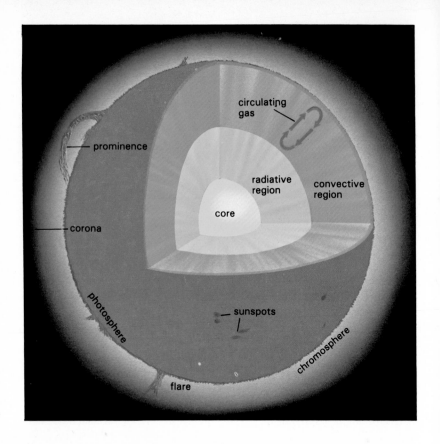

Cutaway of the Sun, showing its internal structure and energy-generating core.

The stellar powerhouse

Stars do not 'burn' in the usual sense of the word. They are powered by nuclear reactions at their centres which turn hydrogen into helium, releasing energy in the process. This is similar to the reaction which occurs in a hydrogen bomb, but in stars the reaction occurs in a more controlled way.

Stars are made largely of hydrogen, which is the simplest and most abundant element in the Universe. For instance, about 70 per cent of the Sun (by weight) is hydrogen, and most of the remainder is helium, the second-simplest and most abundant element. All other elements make up less than two per cent of the Sun's mass. These figures are typical of most other stars. Astronomers have found that the Sun is about average in size and brightness, so we can take the Sun as an example of the life story of many stars.

In the nuclear furnace at the centre of the Sun, atoms of hydrogen are crushed together to make atoms of helium, a process called *fusion*. The temperature at the core of the Sun where this reaction takes place is estimated to be an astoundingly high 15 million°C.

Each second, 600 million tonnes of hydrogen in the Sun is turned into helium, with 4 million tonnes going to produce energy. Even at this prolific rate, the Sun has enough hydrogen stocks to last for about another 5000 million years. The Sun is believed to be in stable middle age, roughly half way through its life cycle.

Star death

Eventually, though, a star starts to run out of hydrogen at its core, having turned it all into helium. Hydrogen-burning then moves out into the surrounding zone. When this happens, the star gets hotter inside, and the result of this extra energy release is that the star swells up in size. As it swells, its surface temperature drops so that it becomes red in colour. The star has become a red giant.

A red giant can be as much as 100 times the size of the present Sun. When our Sun reaches this stage, in billions of years, it will engulf the Earth, thereby ending all life on our planet. For the next stage in the star's development, the helium core also

Death of the Sun – a swollen red giant, baking the Earth to a cinder.

becomes sufficiently heated to ignite and partake in nuclear reactions, this time forming carbon. The extra energy released in these reactions bloats the star still further – so much so that its outer layers drift off into space, forming a stellar smoke ring or *planetary nebula*. Planetary nebulae have nothing to do with planets; they get their name from the fact that through a telescope they resemble the disc of a planet, as you can confirm by your own observations of the planetary nebulae listed in the constellation notes.

At the centre of the expanding shell of gas lies the exposed core of the former red giant star. This small, hot core is known as a white dwarf. A white dwarf star may contain as much mass as the Sun, compressed

Planetary nebula NGC 6781 in Aquila, the discarded outer layers of a former red giant star.

into a ball the size of the Earth. White dwarfs are made of such dense material that a thimbleful of it would weigh several tonnes – more than enough to collapse the sturdiest table!

Since white dwarfs are so small, they are very faint and difficult to spot through amateur telescopes. The most easily observable white dwarf lies in the triple star system, Omicron-2 Eridani. White dwarfs cool off slowly, eventually fading into invisibility. This is predicted to be the final fate of the Sun.

All stars of less than about four times the mass of the Sun go through this life cycle, although at different rates depending on their mass. A star like Sirius, for example, with about twice the mass of the Sun, can live for no longer than 1000 million years, which is one-tenth the Sun's predicted lifetime. At the other end of the scale, red dwarf stars – far smaller and cooler than the Sun – are predicted to live at least 10 times as long as the Sun, because they use up their nuclear fuel so slowly. Red dwarfs, being long-lived, are probably the most abundant stars in the Galaxy, although they are so faint they are difficult to spot.

Death of superstars

Stars with more than about four solar masses die a spectacular death. They turn into red supergiants, larger and brighter even than red giants, and then a series of run-away nuclear reactions sets in at their core. The result is that the star erupts in a gigantic nuclear holocaust known as a *supernova*. In a supernova explosion, the star may flare up in brightness by thousands of millions of times, so that for a few days or weeks it is giving out as much light as an entire galaxy.

As the star erupts, complex nuclear reactions occur which give rise to all the known chemical elements. These atoms are scattered into Space by the explosion to mix with gas clouds and

White dwarf compared with the Earth and a segment of the Sun. Omicron-2 Eridani is a triple star containing a white dwarf.

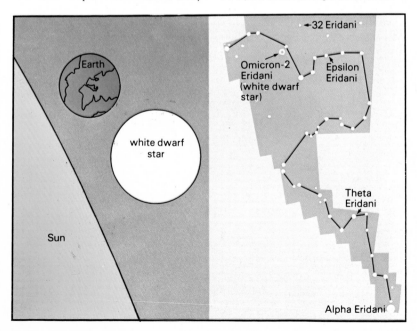

then to be gathered up to make new stars, possibly with planetary systems and even life on these planets. The atoms of which the Earth and our bodies are made are believed to have been formed in ancient supernova explosions before the Sun was born. Therefore, we owe our existence to the death of massive stars.

One famous supernova was seen by Middle Eastern and Oriental astronomers in 1054 AD. Telescopes now reveal, at the site of the supernova, an object known as the Crab Nebula – the shattered remains of the outer layers of the star that exploded. Binoculars or small telescopes show the Crab Nebula as a milky, elongated blur; fascinating detail is brought out on long-exposure photographs.

Some stars blow themselves completely to bits in a supernova. But in many cases the heavy core of the dead star remains as an object even smaller, denser, and more amazing than a white dwarf.

Neutron stars and pulsars

The dense, heavy stellar core left behind by a supernova collapses under the inward pull of its own gravity and the force of the explosion above it, crushing together the protons and electrons of its atoms to form the atomic particles known as neutrons. The object becomes a neutron star. A neutron star contains the mass of two or three Suns squashed into a ball only about 20 kilometres across. A

The Crab Nebula, the shattered remnants of a star which Oriental astronomers saw explode as a supernova in 1054 AD.

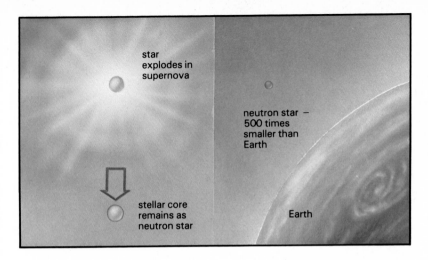

neutron star –
500 times
smaller than
Earth

stellar core
remains as
neutron star

Earth

In a supernova, the core of the exploding star can be compressed to a superdense neutron star, far smaller than the Earth.

thimbleful of neutron star material would weigh a staggering 1000 million tonnes – as much as several thousand fully laden oil supertankers! With such a density, the entire Earth could be fitted into a modest-sized cupboard!

The existence of neutron stars was predicted by theorists as long ago as 1939, but astronomers realized that they would be almost impossible to see because of their tiny size and consequent faintness. But there turned out to be ways of detecting neutron stars other than by seeing them visually.

In 1967, radio astronomers at Cambridge, England, picked up rapid radio pulses coming from several directions in Space. The pulses came as regularly as the ticks of the most accurate clocks, at intervals of a second or so. These flashing radio objects were termed pulsars.

It soon became clear that only a rapidly rotating star could account for the frequency and regularity of the pulses. And the only stars small enough to spin once a second or less were neutron stars. Astronomers now accept that pulsars and neutron stars are the same thing. The neutron star is believed to give out a flash of radiation each time it turns, like a celestial lighthouse.

In 1968, a pulsar was discovered at the centre of the Crab Nebula – proof that pulsars are formed by supernovae. The Crab Pulsar flashes at the astounding rate of 30 times per second, the fastest pulsar known. In 1969, the Crab Pulsar was observed flashing optically at the same rate as the radio pulses. Only one other pulsar, that in the constellation of Vela,

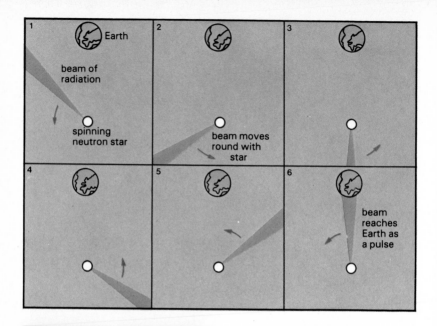

Earth

beam of
radiation

spinning
neutron star

2

beam moves
round with
star

3

4

5

6

beam
reaches
Earth as
a pulse

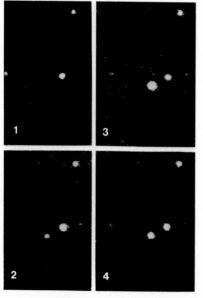

1

2

3

4

Above: A beam of radiation from a
spinning neutron star sweeps over Earth,
causing the effect of a pulsar.

has been observed flashing visibly.
The others are probably too faint.
Over 300 pulsars have now been
detected, flashing from 30 times per
second (the Crab Pulsar) to once
every 4 seconds. Some pulsars have
also been detected at X-ray and
gamma-ray wavelengths by orbiting
satellites.

Black holes

But what if the remnant core of the
supernova has a mass more than
three times that of the Sun? Its own

Left: Sequence of pictures showing the
pulsar in the Crab Nebula flashing on and
off.

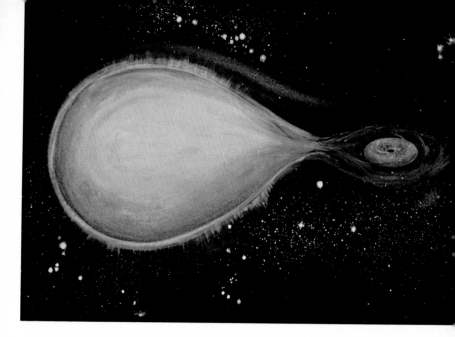

gravity is then so strong that it will not stop at the stage of a neutron star. It keeps shrinking ever smaller and denser until it becomes something far more bizarre – a black hole. A black hole can be most simply defined as a volume of Space in which gravity is so great that nothing can escape, not even light, although things can fall in, as if going down a celestial plug-hole. Therefore a star that collapses into a black hole becomes invisible.

What happens inside a black hole? According to theory, nothing can shore up a collapsing star of more than three solar masses against the crushing force of its own gravity. The star continues shrinking until it reaches a point of zero size and infinitely large density. In effect, the

Cygnus X-1, an X-ray source in which gas from a blue supergiant star is believed to be spiralling into a black hole.

star has shrunk itself out of existence! Such a fate seems to defy logic, but that is what theory predicts. Anyone or anything falling into the black hole would suffer a similar fate. The interior of a black hole is a dead-end in Space and time.

If black holes are invisible, how can we detect them? Fortunately, they give their existence away by swallowing gas from the space around them. It has been mentioned that many stars are double. In cases where one star has died and formed a black hole, it may continue to orbit a companion star that is still shining normally. Gas from the companion star streams into the intense gravitational field of the black hole, heating up to many millions of degrees as it does so before plunging out of sight down the hole. At such temperatures, the gas emits X-rays, which can be detected by observation satellites.

Several possible black holes have been located by X-ray satellites. Most celebrated is the source known as Cygnus X-1, which orbits a faint star, known by its catalogue number of HDE 226868, in the constellation of Cygnus. Observations of this visible star as it moves in orbit with the invisible X-ray emitting companion show that the companion must have a mass of about eight Suns. This is too heavy for it to be a neutron star, so astronomers assume it must be a black hole.

According to the theories, black holes can come in a wide range of sizes. Many astronomers think that enormous black holes, containing the mass of many millions of stars, may reside at the centres of galaxies, and of the mysterious objects known as quasars. Such black holes could originate with the death of one massive star, and grow by the influx of matter. One startling prediction is that 'mini black holes' might exist, having the mass of a mountain compressed into a speck the size of an atomic particle. Such mini black holes could not form today, but might have been produced in the conditions of extreme turbulence that followed the Big Bang explosion which is believed to have marked the origin of the Universe (see page 208). However, there is as yet no evidence for the existence of mini black holes.

Star distances and motions

As we have seen, Cepheid variables provide one means of distance measuring in Space. But the distances of the nearest stars can be measured directly. The position of a nearby star against the sky background appears slightly different as observed at six-monthly intervals, when the Earth is on opposite sides of its orbit. This position shift is the star's parallax. It is too small to be noticed with the naked eye, but can be measured accurately on photographs taken through telescopes.

In addition to parallax, the nearby stars show a systematic change in position over time, known as *proper motion*. This results from the fact that all stars, including the Sun, are orbiting within the Galaxy. The Sun takes about 250 million years to complete

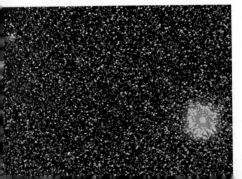

Quasar 3C 273 (right), a possible site of a black hole, seen by NASA's X-ray satellite HEAO-2, also called Einstein.

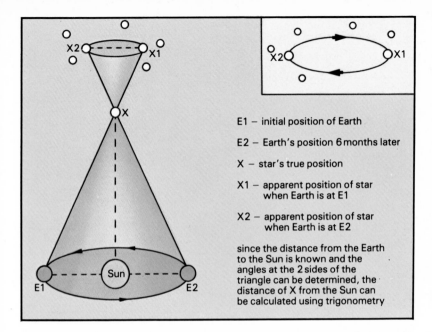

E1 — initial position of Earth

E2 — Earth's position 6 months later

X — star's true position

X1 — apparent position of star when Earth is at E1

X2 — apparent position of star when Earth is at E2

since the distance from the Earth to the Sun is known and the angles at the 2 sides of the triangle can be determined, the distance of X from the Sun can be calculated using trigonometry

Above: Distance of a star can be calculated from its parallax as seen from opposite sides of the Earth's orbit.

one orbit, but other stars are moving at different speeds. Like cars moving at different speeds along a road, some stars appear to move ahead of the Sun while others fall behind.

A star's proper motion is undetectable to the naked eye in a human lifetime, but can be measured accurately on photographs. The proper motions of stars are slowly changing the shapes of the constellations. Far in the future, the sky will look quite different from the way it does today.

Right: Proper motions of stars change the appearance of star groupings with time, as in the case of the Plough.

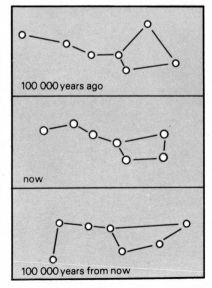

100 000 years ago

now

100 000 years from now

Constellations

Finding your way around the sky

Getting your bearings among the stars can be difficult. The best way of finding your way around is to navigate by reference to well-known constellation figures. They act as a guide to more obscure shapes.

For example, in the northern hemisphere the best starting point is the Plough or Big Dipper of Ursa Major. The bowl of the Dipper points to Polaris, the north Pole Star. On the other side of the pole is the W-shape of Cassiopeia. Extending the pointers of the Dipper in the opposite direction leads to Leo. If you follow the curve of the Dipper's handle, you will find the bright star Arcturus in Bootes. Another good shape to find is the cross of Cygnus. The star Deneb in Cygnus forms the 'Summer Triangle' with Vega in Lyra and Altair in Aquila. The long axis of Cygnus

points to Cassiopeia in one direction and to Ophiuchus in the other. The short axis of Cygnus points away from Lyra to Pegasus.

In the southern hemisphere, the stars Alpha and Beta Centauri in Centaurus point to Crux, the Southern Cross, and the long axis of the cross points to the celestial south pole.

Orion is another good key constellation, visible in both northern and southern hemispheres. Its belt points towards Taurus in one direction and to Canis Major in the other. Betelgeuse in Orion forms a triangle with Procyon in Canis Minor and Sirius in Canis Major. A line from Rigel in Orion through Betelgeuse leads to the constellation Gemini. The stars Castor and Pollux in Gemini point to Capella, the brightest star in the constellation of Auriga.

Although they are in fact far away from the stars of the Milky Way Galaxy, other galaxies can be seen, apparently within the boundaries of the constellations. Such galaxies are therefore included among the objects of interest visible in the constellations. The magnitudes given in this chapter are the apparent magnitudes of the objects.

Below, left: Star clouds in Sagittarius.

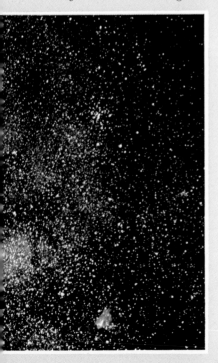

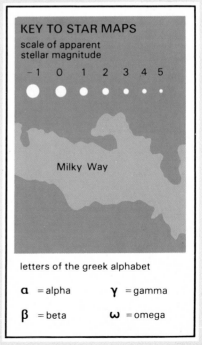

KEY TO STAR MAPS

scale of apparent stellar magnitude

| -1 | 0 | 1 | 2 | 3 | 4 | 5 |

Milky Way

letters of the greek alphabet

α = alpha   γ = gamma

β = beta   ω = omega

HOW THE POLAR STAR MAPS ARE PROJECTED

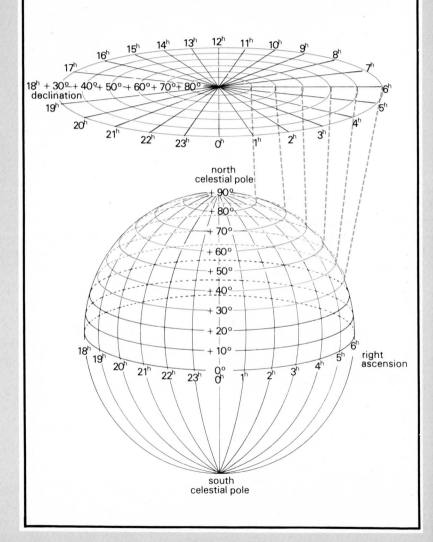

HOW THE SEASONAL STAR MAPS ARE PROJECTED

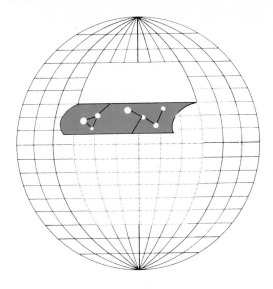

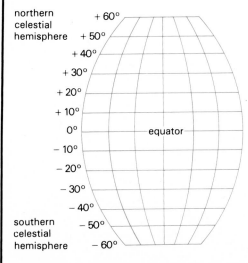

northern
celestial
hemisphere

+ 60°
+ 50°
+ 40°
+ 30°
+ 20°
+ 10°
0°   equator
− 10°
− 20°
− 30°
− 40°

southern
celestial
hemisphere

− 50°
− 60°

(This seasonal division
applies to seasons of the
northern hemisphere of
the Earth. In the southern
hemisphere, 'autumn
constellations', for
example, would be visible
in spring.)

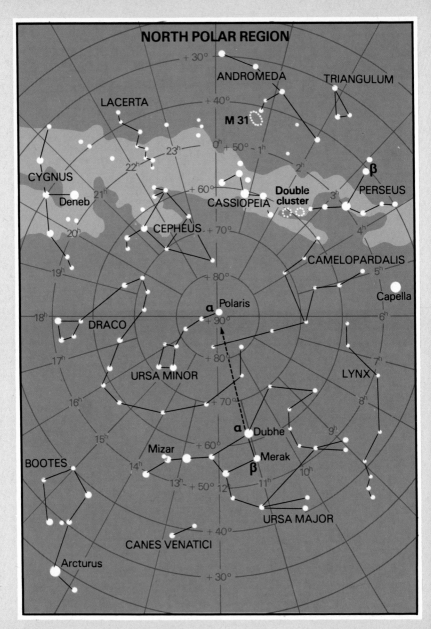

NORTH POLAR REGION

ANDROMEDA

TRIANGULUM

LACERTA

M 31

+30°
+40°
+50°
+60°
+70°
+80°
+90°

β
PERSEUS

Double cluster

CASSIOPEIA

CYGNUS

Deneb

CEPHEUS

CAMELOPARDALIS

Capella

Polaris
α

DRACO

URSA MINOR

LYNX

BOOTES

Mizar

α Dubhe
Merak
β

Arcturus

CANES VENATICI

URSA MAJOR

0h 1h 2h 3h 4h 5h 6h 7h 8h 9h 10h 11h 12h 13h 14h 15h 16h 17h 18h 19h 20h 21h 22h 23h

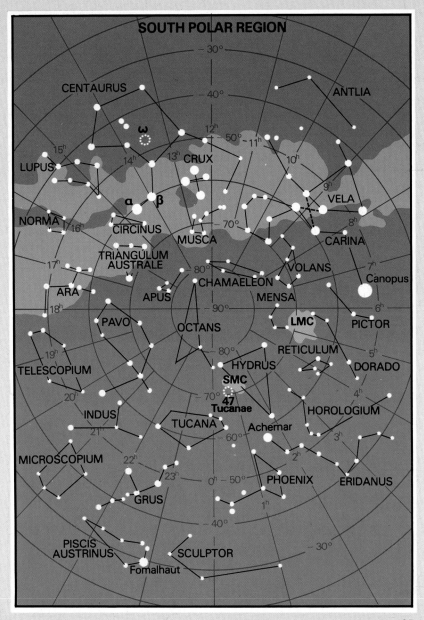

SOUTH POLAR REGION

97

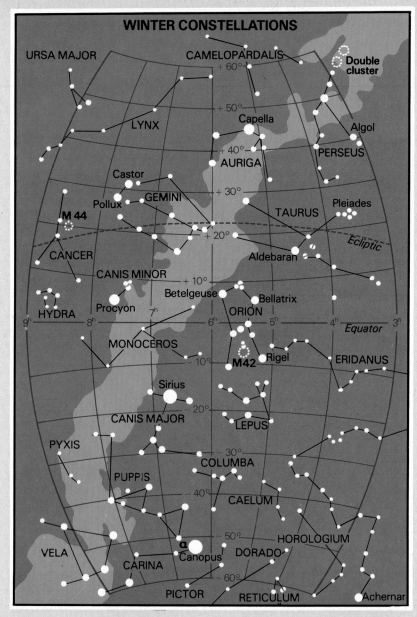

WINTER CONSTELLATIONS

URSA MAJOR

CAMELOPARDALIS

Double cluster

+ 60°

LYNX

+ 50°

Capella

Algol

+ 40°

AURIGA

PERSEUS

Castor

+ 30°

GEMINI

Pollux

Pleiades

TAURUS

M 44

+ 20°

CANCER

Aldebaran

Ecliptic

CANIS MINOR

+ 10°

Betelgeuse

HYDRA

Procyon

Bellatrix

9ʰ   8ʰ   7ʰ   6ʰ   5ʰ   4ʰ   Equator   3ʰ

ORION

MONOCEROS

-10°

M42

Rigel

ERIDANUS

Sirius

-20°

CANIS MAJOR

LEPUS

PYXIS

-30°

COLUMBA

PUPPIS

-40°

CAELUM

VELA

-50°

HOROLOGIUM

α

DORADO

Canopus

CARINA

-60°

PICTOR

RETICULUM

Achernar

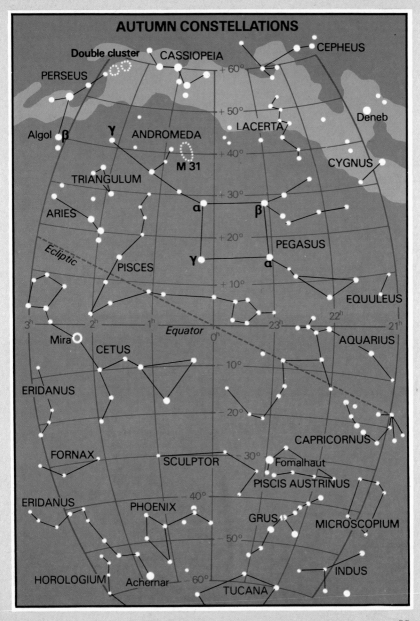

AUTUMN CONSTELLATIONS

Double cluster
CASSIOPEIA
CEPHEUS
PERSEUS
+ 60°
LACERTA
Deneb
Algol β
γ
ANDROMEDA
+ 50°
CYGNUS
+ 40°
M 31
TRIANGULUM
+ 30°
α
β
ARIES
+ 20°
PEGASUS
Ecliptic
γ
α
PISCES
+ 10°
EQUULEUS
3ʰ
2ʰ
1ʰ
Equator
0ʰ
23ʰ
22ʰ
21ʰ
Mira
AQUARIUS
CETUS
– 10°
ERIDANUS
– 20°
CAPRICORNUS
FORNAX
SCULPTOR
– 30°
Fomalhaut
PISCIS AUSTRINUS
ERIDANUS
– 40°
PHOENIX
GRUS
MICROSCOPIUM
– 50°
HOROLOGIUM
Achernar
– 60°
INDUS
TUCANA

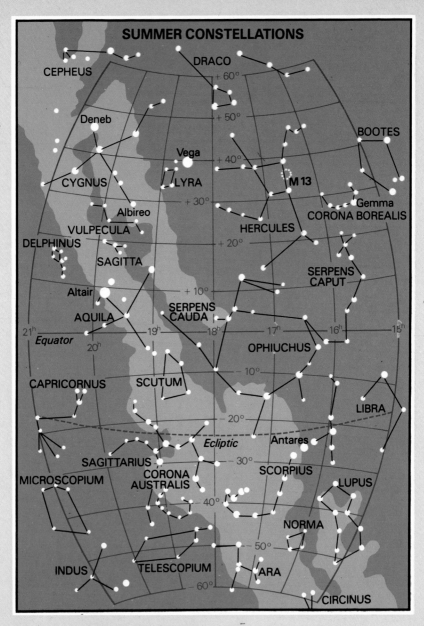

SUMMER CONSTELLATIONS

CEPHEUS

DRACO

+ 60°

+ 50°

Deneb

BOOTES

Vega

+ 40°

CYGNUS

LYRA

M 13

+ 30°

Gemma

Albireo

CORONA BOREALIS

VULPECULA

+ 20°

HERCULES

DELPHINUS

SERPENS
CAPUT

SAGITTA

+ 10°

Altair

SERPENS
CAUDA

AQUILA

21ʰ

19ʰ

18ʰ

17ʰ

16ʰ

15ʰ

Equator

20ʰ

OPHIUCHUS

CAPRICORNUS

SCUTUM

− 10°

LIBRA

− 20°

Ecliptic

Antares

SAGITTARIUS

− 30°

SCORPIUS

MICROSCOPIUM

CORONA
AUSTRALIS

LUPUS

− 40°

NORMA

− 50°

INDUS

TELESCOPIUM

ARA

− 60°

CIRCINUS

100

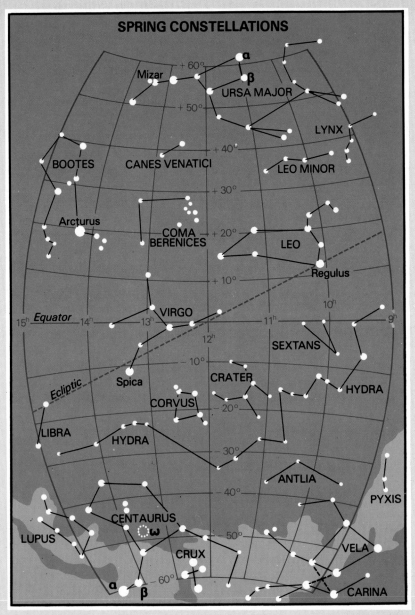

SPRING CONSTELLATIONS

α

β

Mizar

URSA MAJOR

+ 60°

+ 50°

LYNX

+ 40°

BOOTES

CANES VENATICI

LEO MINOR

+ 30°

Arcturus

+ 20°

COMA
BERENICES

LEO

+ 10°

Regulus

10ʰ

Equator

15ʰ   14ʰ   13ʰ   VIRGO

11ʰ

9ʰ

12ʰ

SEXTANS

10°

CRATER

Ecliptic

Spica

HYDRA

20°

CORVUS

LIBRA

HYDRA

30°

ANTLIA

40°

PYXIS

LUPUS

CENTAURUS   ω

50°

VELA

CRUX

60°

α   **β**

CARINA

101

Andromeda

A major constellation in the northern hemisphere of the sky, representing the beautiful daughter of Queen Cassiopeia and King Cepheus. In a popular myth, Andromeda was chained to a rock and would have been devoured by the sea monster Cetus, but was saved in the nick of time by Perseus. These other charac-' ters in the Andromeda legend are represented by other constellations that lie nearby in the sky.

The constellation's most celebrated feature is the Andromeda Galaxy, a spiral galaxy similar to our own Milky Way; it is the farthest object visible to the naked eye. The star Alpha Andromeda, also known as Alpheratz or Sirrah, has been 'borrowed' by neighbouring Pegasus to form one corner of the famous Square of Pegasus.

Objects of interest
Gamma Andromedae is one of the most beautiful double stars in the sky. Small telescopes show it to consist of yellow and blue components of magnitudes 2·3 and 5·5.

M 31, also known as NGC 224, is the Andromeda Galaxy, a massive spiral of stars 2·2 million light years away. This twin of our Milky Way can be studied through all sizes of instrument. It is easily found by following two stars that lead from Beta Andromedae. The Andromeda Galaxy is visible to the naked eye as an elongated smudge, but is more prominent when seen through binoculars. Using telescopes with low magnification, its faint outer reaches can be traced out to a degree or more from the brighter core. Also visible are two satellite galaxies, similar to the Magellanic Clouds which accompany the Milky Way.
NGC 7662 is one of the brightest planetary nebulae, of magnitude 8·5, and is visible through small telescopes as a fuzzy, greenish dot like an out-of-focus star.

Antlia the air pump

A small, faint constellation in the southern hemisphere of the sky. It was

Andromeda Galaxy and its two satellites, M 32 (left) and NGC 205 (lower right).

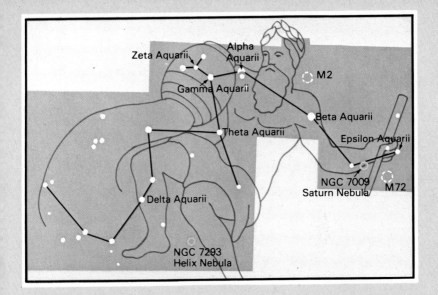

Depiction of the constellation Aquarius, seen as a figure pouring water from a jar.

introduced by Nicolas Louis de Lacaille. The name commemorates the air pump made by the English physicist Robert Boyle. It contains no stars brighter than fourth magnitude.

Object of interest
NGC 3132 is a prominent planetary nebula lying on the border of Antlia with the constellation Vela. It is similar in size to the famous Ring Nebula in Lyra, but brighter. Telescopes show it to be elliptical in shape, and of eighth magnitude. The complex structure of NGC 3132 has led to the name 'the Eight-burst' nebula.

Apus the bird of paradise

An unimpressive constellation near the south pole of the sky, representing the exotic bird of paradise. Apus became a recognized constellation in 1603 when it was shown on a star map by the German astronomer Johann

Bayer, but its introduction was actually due to Dutch seamen. The constellation's brightest stars are of only fourth magnitude, and Apus contains no objects of particular interest.

Aquarius the water carrier

A major constellation in the equatorial region of the sky, popularly depicted as a man or boy pouring water from a jar. This constellation's association with water dates back to the dawn of civilization. Aquarius is surrounded by other 'watery' constellations, including Pisces and Capricornus. Aquarius is the 11th constellation of the Zodiac, and the Sun passes through it from late February to early March.

Three meteor showers radiate from Aquarius each year. The strongest shower is the Delta Aquarids, which

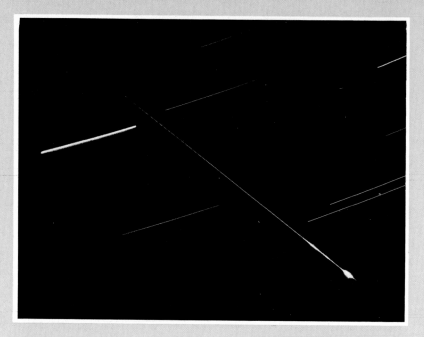

reach a maximum of about 35 meteors an hour on 28 July each year; on 5 May the Eta Aquarids peak at around 20 meteors an hour; while the weakest shower is the Iota Aquarids, with a maximum of only 6 meteors an hour around 6 August. Each shower is named after the bright star closest to the point from which the meteors appear to radiate.

Objects of interest
Zeta Aquarii is a close pair of identical white stars each of magnitude 4·5, requiring telescopes of at least 75 millimetres (3 inches) aperture and high magnification to separate the two.
M 2 (NGC 7089) is a sixth-magnitude globular cluster visible as a round, fuzzy patch through binoculars or small telescopes.
NGC 7009, the Saturn Nebula, is an

Aquarid meteor flaring and exploding as it burned up in the atmosphere.

eighth-magnitude planetary nebula, visible as a fuzzy greenish star through small telescopes. Large telescopes show it to possess extended arms, like the rings of Saturn seen edge-on, which give rise to its popular name.
NGC 7293, the Helix Nebula, is the largest planetary nebula, with an apparent diameter half that of the Moon, but it is very faint. It is best seen through binoculars or telescopes which have very low magnification, and it appears as a circular patch of misty light. Its appearance is much more spectacular on long-exposure photographs.

Above right: Saturn Nebula, NGC 7009.
Right: The Helix Nebula, NGC 7293.
Both are planetary nebulae in Aquarius.

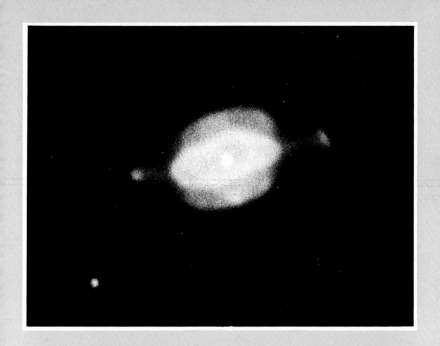

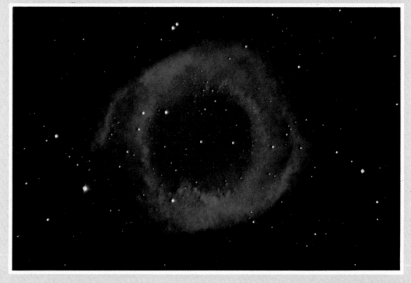

Aquila the eagle

A constellation in the equatorial region of the sky, easily located by its brightest star, Altair, which forms the so-called 'Summer Triangle' with the stars Vega, in the constellation Lyra, and Deneb, in Cygnus. Aquila represents the eagle that was a companion of the Roman god Jupiter. It appears to be flying down the Milky Way. Aquila contains rich star fields to be seen through binoculars, particularly towards the border with Scutum.

Objects of interest
Alpha Aquilae (Altair, from the Arabic for flying eagle) is a brilliant white star of magnitude 0·8. It lies only 16 light years away, making it one of the Sun's closest stellar neighbours.
Eta Aquilae is the third-brightest Cepheid variable star, outshone only by Polaris and Delta Cephei itself. It

varies between magnitudes 3·7 and 4·5 every 7 days 4 hours 15 minutes.

Ara the altar

A constellation of the southern hemisphere of the sky, described as a sacrificial altar or as the altar on which the gods swore an oath of allegiance. Its brightest stars are of third magnitude, and it lies in a rich part of the Milky Way, south of Scorpius.

Objects of interest
NGC 6193 is a cluster, visible through binoculars, of about 30 stars. The brightest stars are of sixth magnitude and the cluster is embedded in nebulosity.
NGC 6397 is a seventh-magnitude globular cluster visible through bino-

Zeta Aurigae consists of an orange supergiant and a smaller blue companion.

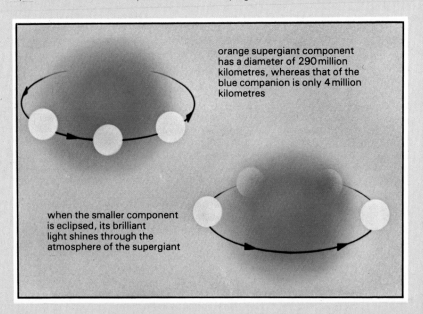

orange supergiant component has a diameter of 290 million kilometres, whereas that of the blue companion is only 4 million kilometres

when the smaller component is eclipsed, its brilliant light shines through the atmosphere of the supergiant

culars and small telescopes. Investigation has shown this to be the closest known globular cluster to us, 8000 light years away.

Aries the ram

An unimpressive but important constellation of the northern celestial hemisphere, representing the ram with the golden fleece which in legend was sought by Jason and the Argonauts. Its brightest star, called Hamal from the Arabic for sheep, is of magnitude 2·2. Aries is the first constellation of the Zodiac. The Sun is within the constellation's boundaries from late April to mid May.

Object of interest
Gamma Arietis consists of a pair of fifth-magnitude white stars, easily distinguished through small telescopes.

Auriga the charioteer

A large and prominent constellation of the northern celestial hemisphere, represented as a young man driving a wagon or chariot, accompanied by a she-goat (the star Capella at the charioteer's left shoulder) and her two kids. The star Gamma Aurigae is shared with the constellation Taurus, the bull, and it is more usually referred to as Beta Tauri. Auriga contains several attractive star clusters.

Objects of interest
Alpha Aurigae (Capella, meaning little she-goat) is a brilliant yellow star of magnitude 0·1, the seventh-brightest star in the sky. It is 45 light years away.
Epsilon Aurigae is a yellow supergiant star which normally shines at magnitude 3·4. But every 27 years it is

M 37 is a showpiece star cluster in Auriga, easily visible through binoculars.

eclipsed by a darker companion; according to one theory, this companion may be a star surrounded by a ring of dark dust from which a planetary system is forming.
Zeta Aurigae is another astounding eclipsing binary, in which a supergiant orange star is orbited every 2 years 8 months by a small, hot blue star.
M 36 (NGC 1960) is a small star cluster visible through binoculars and small telescopes.
M 37 (NGC 1912) is the largest and brightest star cluster in Auriga, easily visible through binoculars. Telescopes reveal M 37 as a dense field of faint stars with a brighter orange star at the centre.

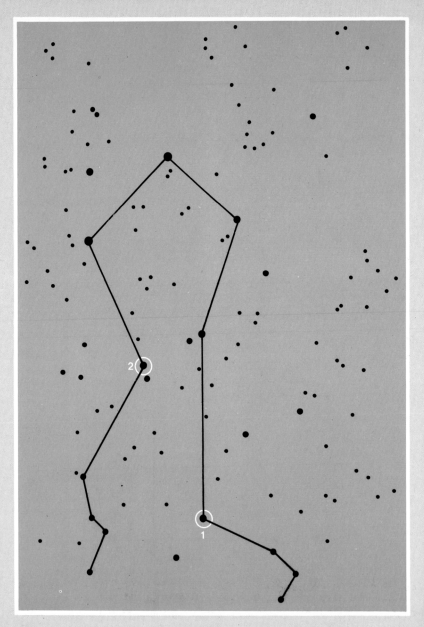

Bootes the herdsman

A large constellation, made prominent by its leading star, Arcturus, which is the brightest star in the northern hemisphere of the sky and is noticeably orange coloured. Bootes represents a herdsman driving a bear (Ursa Major) around the sky. The herdsman's dogs are represented by the neighbouring constellation Canes Venatici. Bootes is noted for its double stars. The radiant point of the year's most prolific meteor shower, the Quadrantids, lies within the northern part of Bootes, an area once occupied by the defunct constellation of Quadrans, from which the shower takes its name. The Quadrantids reach their peak of over 100 meteors an hour on 3 or 4 January each year.

Objects of interest
Alpha Bootis (Arcturus, the bear-keeper) is a red giant star, 27 times the Sun's diameter, of magnitude −0·06, the fourth-brightest star in the entire sky. It lies 36 light years away.
Epsilon Bootis (Izar, meaning girdle) is a celebrated close double star requiring a telescope with at least 75 millimetres (3 inches) aperture with high magnification and steady air to distinguish the stars. The component stars are orange and blue-green, of magnitudes 2·7 and 5·1. The striking colour contrast of the pair has led to its alternative name of Pulcherrima, 'most beautiful'.
Mu Bootis (Alkalurops, staff or crook) appears through binoculars as a double star of magnitudes 4·3 and

Left: Bootes and some of its main stars.
1: Alpha Bootis (Arcturus), magnitude −0·1. **2**: Epsilon Bootis, the celebrated double. The star directly beneath Epsilon is 34 Bootis, an entirely separate star and not Epsilon's close companion.

6·5. Telescopes of 75 millimetres (3 inches) aperture split the fainter component into two yellow stars of seventh magnitude.
Xi Bootis is a showpiece double star to be seen through small telescopes. It consists of yellow and orange stars of magnitudes 4·8 and 6·9.

Caelum the chisel

A small, obscure constellation in the south celestial hemisphere, introduced by Lacaille during his mapping of the southern sky. It contains no star brighter than magnitude 4·5, and virtually nothing of any interest.

Camelopardalis the giraffe

A faint but extensive constellation in the northern hemisphere of the sky. Camelopardalis (also given as Camelopardus) became a generally recognized constellation in 1624 when it was shown in a book by the German mathematician Jakob Bartsch (a son-in-law of Johannes Kepler), although it had probably been introduced by others previously. Its brightest star is of the fourth magnitude, and despite its size Camelopardalis contains little of interest to casual observers.

Cancer the crab

The fourth constellation of the Zodiac, lying in the northern hemisphere of the sky. Cancer is said to represent the crab which pinched the toes of the great hero Hercules and was crushed underfoot. As befits such a minor mythological figure, Cancer is the faintest constellation of the Zodiac, its brightest stars being of only the fourth magnitude. The Sun passes through

M 44 is a famous star cluster in Cancer, and is known as Praesepe or the Beehive cluster. It is prominent in binoculars.

the constellation from late July to mid August.

Objects of interest

Zeta Cancri is a double star, with components of magnitudes 5·1 and 6·0, easily seen through small telescopes. The brighter component has a close, sixth-magnitude companion which requires apertures of at least 100 millimetres (4 inches) to be visible.

Iota Cancri is a magnitude 4·2 yellow star with a companion of magnitude 6·6 visible through small telescopes or even good binoculars.

M 44 (NGC 2632) is a large and loose star cluster containing at least 75 members visible through amateur tele-

scopes. It is called Praesepe, a name which means the Manger, although a more popular title is 'Beehive Cluster'. To the naked eye Praesepe appears as a misty patch, and is easily seen through binoculars.

M 67 (NGC 2682) is a fainter but richer cluster than M 44, visible through binoculars but needing a 100-millimetre (4-inch) telescope to resolve it into individual stars.

Canes Venatici
the hunting dogs

A faint but interesting constellation between Ursa Major and Bootes in the northern hemisphere of the sky, introduced in 1690 by the Polish astronomer Johannes Hevelius. It represents the dogs Chara and Asterion belonging to the herdsman Bootes.

Objects of interest

Alpha Canum Venaticorum is popularly known as Cor Caroli, meaning 'Charles' heart' — a reference to the executed King Charles I of England. Small telescopes separate it easily into two components of magnitudes 2·9 and 5·4.

M 3 (NGC 5272) is a globular cluster visible through binoculars and small telescopes.

M 51 (NGC 5194) is a celebrated spiral galaxy, known as 'the Whirlpool'. It was the first galaxy in which spiral structure was detected, by Lord Rosse in 1845. Photographs show it as a face-on spiral with a satellite galaxy at the end of one of its arms, but it is a faint and disappointing sight through small telescopes.

The Whirlpool Galaxy, M 51, in Canes Venatici, is a spiral galaxy with a satellite galaxy at the end of one arm.

Sirius, the brightest star in the sky, has a faint white dwarf companion, just visible as a small dot in this photograph.

Canis Major the greater dog

A brilliant constellation in the southern hemisphere of the sky, representing one of the two dogs of Orion (the other dog is Canis Minor). Canis Major is unmistakable, for it contains Sirius, the brightest star in the entire sky. The ancient Egyptians represented Sirius by the symbol for a dog, and based their calendar on the star's yearly motion around the sky.

Objects of interest
Alpha Canis Majoris (Sirius) is a brilliant white star, magnitude −1·5, lying 8·7 light years away; it is therefore the fifth closest star to the Sun. Sirius appears as the brightest star in the sky, although there are some stars more brilliant but farther away. It has a faint white-dwarf companion which orbits it every 50 years, visible only through large telescopes.
M41 (NGC 2287) is a star cluster just visible to the naked eye, and easily seen through binoculars and small telescopes.

Canis Minor the lesser dog

A small constellation just north of the celestial equator representing the second of the two dogs of Orion, the other being Canis Major. But for its brightest star, Procyon, the eighth-brightest star in the entire sky, the constellation would be totally unremarkable.

Object of interest
Alpha Canis Minoris (Procyon) is a brilliant white star of magnitude 0·3, lying 11 light years from us (which means it is relatively close to the Sun). Like its near-neighbour Sirius, it has a white dwarf companion star visible only through large telescopes.

Capricornus the sea goat

A constellation of the southern celestial hemisphere, representing a mythical creature with the body of a goat and the tail of a fish. Such amphibious creatures were common in ancient middle-eastern legends; the constellation's true origin is lost in the mists of antiquity. Capricornus is the tenth constellation of the Zodiac. The Sun passes through its boundaries from late January to mid February.

Objects of interest
Alpha Capricorni (Algedi, meaning goat or ibex) consists of a pair of stars, visible separately with the naked eye or binoculars, of magnitudes 3·8 and 4·6. They are not related, but lie 115 and 1100 light years away respectively, so appear in the same line of sight purely by chance.
Beta Capricorni, magnitude 3·3, is a golden-yellow star with a sixth-magnitude companion visible through binoculars or small telescopes.

Carina the keel

Carina once formed part of the much larger southern hemisphere constellation of Argo Navis, the ship of Jason and the Argonauts, until that constel- lation was sub-divided in the 1750s by the celestial cartographer, Nicolas Louis de Lacaille. The other sections of the ship are Puppis, Pyxis, and Vela. Carina lies in a rich region of the Milky Way. The stars Iota and Epsilon Carinae, together with Kappa and Delta Velorum, form the so-called 'false cross', sometimes mistaken for the true Southern Cross.

Objects of interest
Alpha Carinae (Canopus) is a yellow-white supergiant star of magnitude −0·7, the second brightest star in the entire sky. (Sirius is brightest of all.) Canopus is 110 light years away.
Eta Carinae is a peculiar star given to wild and unpredictable fluctuations in brightness. It is currently of sixth magnitude, but in the past has flared up to

Glowing nebulosity around the peculiar eruptive, variable star Eta Carinae.

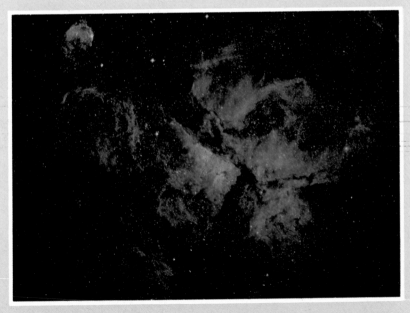

113

as bright as magnitude −1. Eta Carinae lies within a large, bright nebula known as NGC 3372, visible to the naked eye and glorious through binoculars. One dark patch near the centre of the nebula is known as 'the Keyhole' because of its distinctive shape. **NGC 3532** is a large and bright star cluster visible to the naked eye. Binoculars and small telescopes reveal a widespread scattering of stars.

Cassiopeia

One of the most distinctive constellations, easily recognized by its W-shape, lying in the far northern part of the sky. Cassiopeia represents a mythological Queen of Egypt, wife of King Cepheus and mother of Andromeda. She is depicted sitting in a chair, which is the shape formed by the constellation's five brightest stars. Cassiopeia lies in the Milky Way.

Objects of interest
Gamma Cassiopeiae, the central star of the W-shape, is a giant blue star which occasionally throws off shells

Cassiopeia, with stars of interest ringed.
1: Gamma. **2**: Eta. **3**: Iota.

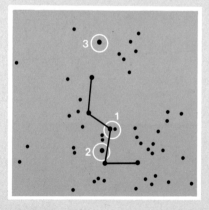

of gas into space, thereby causing sudden fluctuations in its brightness. It is normally about magnitude 2·5, but it can vary between magnitudes 1·6 and 3.
Eta Cassiopeiae is a beautiful double star to be seen through small telescopes, and consists of yellow and red components of magnitudes 3·6 and 7·5.
Iota Cassiopeiae appears through small telescopes as a double star of magnitudes 4·6 and 8. Telescopes with apertures of 100 millimetres (4 inches) and high magnification show that the brighter star has a close seventh-magnitude companion, making this a noteworthy triple star.
M 52 (NGC 7654) is a cluster of over 100 stars, visible through binoculars.

Centaurus the centaur

A large and brilliant constellation in the southern hemisphere of the sky, containing the nearest star to the Sun, Alpha Centauri (actually a triple star), and the largest and brightest globular cluster, Omega Centauri. The constellation represents the centaur of Greek mythology, half man, half horse. Centaurus lies in a rich part of the Milky Way.

Objects of interest
Alpha Centauri (Rigil Kentaurus) is the closest star to the Sun, being 4·3 light years away. To the naked eye it shines at magnitude −0·3, but small telescopes reveal it to consist of two yellow stars of magnitudes 0·0 and 1·4, which orbit each other every 80 years. A faint third star also belongs to the Alpha Centauri system. This star is a red dwarf of magnitude 11. Since it is about one-tenth of a light year closer to us than the other components of Alpha Centauri, it is popularly called Proxima Centauri.

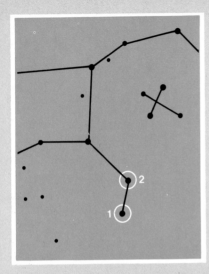

Left: Alpha and Beta Centauri (labelled 1 and 2 respectively) point towards the Southern Cross (upper right of picture).

Beta Centauri is a blue giant of magnitude 0·6. A line drawn through Alpha and Beta Centauri points to Crux, the Southern Cross.

Omega Centauri is the finest globular cluster in the sky, visible to the naked eye like a fuzzy star of fourth magnitude, covering an area two-thirds that of the full Moon. Small telescopes or even binoculars reveal individual bright stars in the outer regions of the cluster.

Below: Omega Centauri is the finest globular cluster in the sky. Amateur telescopes reveal the brightest individual stars dotted around its outer regions.

Cepheus the king

A large constellation extending to the north pole of the sky, representing a mythological king of Egypt, the husband of Cassiopeia and father of Andromeda. The constellation is noted for its double and variable stars, particularly Delta Cephei, prototype of the celebrated Cepheid variables.

Objects of interest
Beta Cephei is a giant blue star of magnitude 3·3 with a wide eighth-magnitude companion visible through small telescopes.
Delta Cephei is both a double and a variable star. It is a cream-coloured supergiant that varies between magnitudes 3·6 and 4·3 every 5 days 9 hours as a result of pulsations in its size. Binoculars show it to have a seventh-magnitude blue companion.
Mu Cephei is a supergiant red star, called the 'garnet star' by Sir William Herschel because of its strong red tint, which is prominent through binoculars. It varies irregularly between magnitudes 3·6 and 5·1.

Cetus the whale

The fourth-largest constellation in the sky, sprawling across the celestial equator on the shores of Eridanus, the river. In mythology, Cetus was the monster that threatened to devour Andromeda. Beta Ceti, the brightest star, is of magnitude 2·2, but the rest of the constellation is much fainter.

Objects of interest
Gamma Ceti is a close yellow and blue duo, magnitudes 3·7 and 6·4, requiring a telescope with at least 60 millimetres (2·4 inches) aperture and high magnification to resolve them.

Stars of interest in Cepheus. **1**: Beta Cephei. **2**: Delta Cephei. **3**: Mu Cephei.

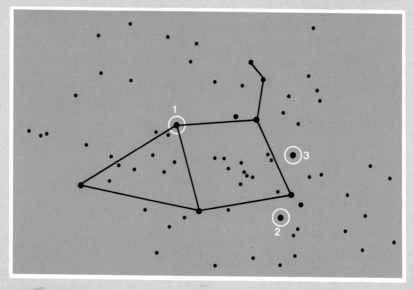

The Black Eye Galaxy, M 64, is a spiral with a dark dust cloud near its centre.

Omicron Ceti (Mira, the wonderful) is the classic example of a red giant that pulsates in size and brightness over a long period. Mira varies between third and ninth magnitude about every 11 months. Its variability was first noted by the Dutch astronomer David Fabricius in 1596, making it the first variable star (apart from novae) to be discovered.

Tau Ceti is a yellow star very similar to the Sun, and some astronomers speculate that it may have planets. It has featured prominently in science fiction, and is a popular target for searches to detect radio messages from other beings in space. Tau Ceti is one of the Sun's closest neighbours, lying 12 light years away, and is of magnitude 3·7.

Chamaeleon the chamaeleon

A constellation near the south pole of the sky and introduced in 1603 by Bayer. None of its stars is brighter than fourth magnitude, and the constellation has little to distinguish it.

Circinus the compasses

The fourth-smallest constellation in the sky, lying in the southern hemisphere next to Centaurus. Circinus was introduced by Lacaille, and contains nothing to interest the casual observer.

Columba the dove

A small and unremarkable constellation of the southern celestial hemisphere, representing the dove that was released from Noah's Ark. Bayer first showed it on his star map of 1603, but it had probably been named by Dutch navigators before him.

Coma Berenices
Berenice's hair

An extremely faint constellation in the northern hemisphere of the sky, but of importance to astronomers because it contains a rich field of distant galaxies. The constellation represents the hair of Queen Berenice of Egypt, who cut off her golden tresses in gratitude to the gods for the safe return of her husband from battle.

Object of interest
M 64 (NGC 4826) is a ninth-magnitude spiral galaxy just visible as a smudge through small amateur instruments. Larger telescopes show a dark cloud of dust surrounding the galaxy's central core which gives rise to this object's popular name of 'the Black-eye Galaxy'.

Corona Australis
the southern crown

A faint arc of stars of fourth magnitude and less in the southern hemisphere of the sky. In one myth, the constellation forms the crown worn by the centaur Sagittarius. Corona Australis contains no notable objects.

Corona Borealis
the northern crown

A noticeable arc of stars in the northern hemisphere of the sky, said to be the crown of Princess Ariadne of Crete. The crown's brightest star, called Gemma, is of magnitude 2·3, but the others are all much fainter.

Objects of interest
Zeta Coronae Borealis is a pair of blue stars of magnitudes 5·1 and 6·0, distinguishable through small telescopes.
R Coronae Borealis is a sixth-magnitude star lying within the arc of the northern crown, which occasionally undergoes catastrophic drops in brightness, to as faint as magnitude 14. These unpredictable declines in the light output of R Coronae Borealis occur every few years, and are believed to be due to the accumulation of carbon 'soot' in the star's outer layers.
T Coronae Borealis, known as the Blaze Star, is a recurrent nova which erupted from its usual 10th magnitude to second magnitude in 1866 and 1946. Another surge in brightness can occur at any time.

Corvus the crow

A constellation of the southern celestial hemisphere, supposedly representing a greedy crow that wasted time eating figs instead of carrying out its errand of fetching water in a cup. The cup is represented by the neighbouring constellation Crater.

Object of interest
Delta Corvi is a double star easily seen with small telescopes, and consists of components of magnitudes 3·1 and 8·4.

Crater the cup

A faint and unimpressive neighbour of Corvus in the southern hemisphere of the sky, containing nothing of note.

Crux the Southern Cross

The smallest constellation in the sky, but one of the most distinctive. It lies in the south celestial hemisphere next to the brilliant Centaurus, of which it originally formed a part. It seems to have been made into a separate constellation sometime in the 16th century by seamen and other travellers. Crux lies in a rich part of the Milky Way, and includes a dark obscuring cloud known as 'the Coalsack'.

Objects of interest
Alpha Crucis (Acrux) appears to the naked eye as a brilliant blue-white star of magnitude 0·8, but small telescopes show it to be double, with components of magnitudes 1·6 and 2·1. Alpha Crucis is about 300 light years away.
NGC 4755, the Kappa Crucis star cluster, is a bright group of at least 50 stars, visible to the naked eye as a fuzzy patch. Its glittering appearance through telescopes has led to the popular name 'the Jewel Box'.
The Coalsack Nebula is a wedge-shaped cloud of dark dust seen silhouetted against the rich star fields of

the Milky Way, giving the appearance of a 'hole' in the Milky Way. The Coalsack measures nearly 7° by 5°, and spills over into the neighbouring constellations of Centaurus and Musca.

Dark Coalsack Nebula, Kappa Crucis star cluster (ringed) and the Southern Cross.

The Coalsack is about 500 light years away.

Cygnus the swan

A large and prominent constellation of the northern hemisphere of the sky, representing a swan flying along the Milky Way. In mythology, the god Zeus turned himself into a swan for a

Left: Glowing filaments of the Veil Nebula in Cygnus, believed to be the shattered remains of a star that exploded as a supernova about 60 000 years ago.

secret visit to Queen Leda of Sparta; the result of their union was Pollux, one of the heavenly twins of Gemini. Another legend identifies Cygnus with the musician Orpheus, who was turned into a swan and placed in the sky next to his favourite instrument, the harp or lyre (represented by the neighbouring constellation of Lyra).

The distinctive cross-shape of Cygnus has led to its popular alternative name of the Northern Cross. Cygnus contains a dark cloud of dust, known as 'the Northern Coalsack', which produces a rift in the Milky Way. The brightest star in Cygnus, Deneb, forms one corner of the famous Summer Triangle of stars, which is completed by Vega in Lyra and Altair in Aquila. Near the star Eta Cygni lies the celebrated X-ray source Cygnus X-1, believed to mark the site of a black hole. Near Epsilon Cygni, long arcs of glowing gas known as the Veil Nebula are revealed by large telescopes; this gas is believed to have been thrown off by a star which exploded as a supernova 60 000 years ago.

Objects of interest

Alpha Cygni (Deneb, the swan's tail) is one of the most luminous stars known. Although lying 1500 light years away, it still appears in our skies as magnitude 1·3. Its actual light output must be about 60 000 times that of our Sun.

Beta Cygni (Albireo) is one of the most famous double stars in the sky, celebrated for its beautiful colour contrast and its clear visibility. It consists of yellow and blue components of magnitudes 3·2 and 5·4, just separable through good binoculars, and a glorious sight through any amateur telescope.

Delta Cygni is a close pair of stars of magnitudes 3·0 and 6·5, needing a 100-millimetre (4-inch) aperture and high magnification telescope to distinguish them.

Cygnus, showing three stars of interest. **1**: Alpha Cygni (Deneb). **2**: Beta Cygni (Albireo). **3**: Delta Cygni.

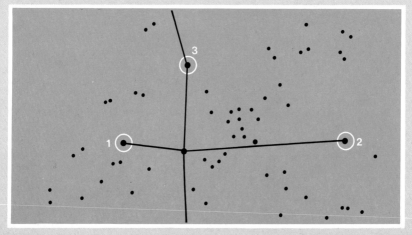

Above: 61 Cygni is an attractive double star, easily seen through small telescopes.

Omicron-1 Cygni is an attractive pair of orange and blue stars, magnitudes 4 and 5, which can be seen through binoculars. Good binoculars or a small telescope show another blue star, of magnitude 7, closer to the brighter (orange) component.

61 Cygni is a famous double star, consisting of twin orange components of magnitudes 5·2 and 6·0, easily separated through small telescopes. 61 Cygni is among the closest stars to the Sun, lying 11·2 light years away, and was in fact the first star to have its parallax measured, by the German astronomer Friedrich Wilhelm Bessel in 1838.

NGC 6826 is an eighth-magnitude planetary nebula known as 'the Blinking Planetary' because it appears to blink on and off as one looks at it. It is visible as a pale blue disc through 75-millimetre (3-inch) telescopes.

NGC 7000 is a faint gas cloud near Deneb known as 'the North American Nebula' because its shape resembles the continent of North America. It can be detected through good binoculars on a clear night, but is best seen on long-exposure photographs.

Delphinus the dolphin

A compact and attractive constellation of the northern hemisphere of the sky, shaped like a small kite with a tail. It represents that charming marine creature, the dolphin, which so often accompanies vessels at sea. Delphinus lies in a rich area of the Milky Way,

Below: The North American Nebula is a gas cloud named because of its shape.

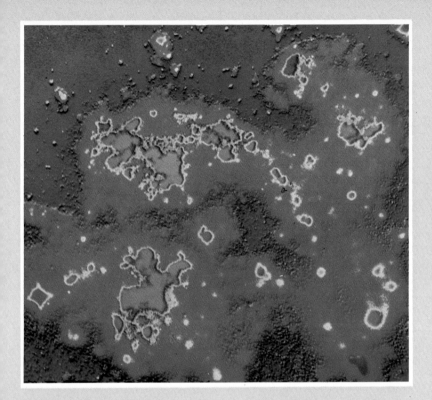

The Large Magellanic Cloud is a satellite galaxy of the Milky Way. Here it is photographed in ultraviolet light from the surface of the Moon.

and like the neighbouring constellations Sagitta and Vulpecula is a common area for novae.

Object of interest
Gamma Delphini is a magnificent pair of golden and yellow stars to be seen through small telescopes, magnitudes 4·5 and 5·5.

Dorado the goldfish

A faint constellation of the southern hemisphere of the sky, introduced by Bayer. It would be unremarkable but for the fact that it contains the Large Magellanic Cloud, one of two satellite galaxies of our own Milky Way. The other satellite, the Small Magellanic Cloud, lies 20° away in Tucana. Dorado is sometimes also known as 'the Swordfish'.

Objects of interest
Large Magellanic Cloud. This mini-galaxy 160 000 light years from us contains perhaps 10 000 million stars, plus several bright nebulae, notably the Tarantula Nebula. The Large Magellanic Cloud appears to the

naked eye as a hazy cloud, like a detached part of the Milky Way, 6° across (12 times the apparent width of the full Moon). Binoculars and small telescopes resolve individual stars and clusters in the Large Magellanic Cloud.

Tarantula Nebula, also known as NGC 2070 or 30 Doradus, is a luminous cloud of gas in the Large Magellanic Cloud, visible to the naked eye. Its long, looping streamers, like the legs of a spider, have given rise to the popular name of the Tarantula. The Tarantula is the largest known nebula in the Universe. If it were as close as the Orion Nebula, it would fill the entire constellation of Orion, and shine with three times the light of the planet Venus — bright enough to cast shadows!

Tarantula Nebula, a cloud of glowing gas in the Large Magellanic Cloud.

legend sees it as the dragon slain by Hercules, who has his foot on the dragon's head.

Gamma Draconis, magnitude 2·4, is the brightest star in the constellation. Alpha Draconis (Thuban), magnitude 3·6, was the Pole Star nearly 5000 years ago, but has lost that distinction to the present Polaris because of the wobble of the Earth in space known as precession.

Draco the dragon

A large but faint constellation which straggles around the north pole of the sky. In one story, Draco represents a dragon guarding the pole; another

Objects of interest

Mu Draconis is a delicate pair of fifth-magnitude cream-coloured stars requiring 100 millimetres (4 inches) aperture and high power telescopes to distinguish them.

Nu Draconis is a fine duo of white stars, each of magnitude 5, visible through binoculars.

16-17 Draconis is a binocular pair of near-identical fifth-magnitude blue-white stars. Telescopes of 60 millimetres (2·4 inches), or more, aperture show that one star has a closer sixth-magnitude companion, making this an interesting triple system.

Equuleus
the foal or little horse

The second-smallest constellation in the sky, and very faint; it contains only one star as bright as the fourth magnitude. Equuleus lies just north of the celestial equator, next to the larger horse, Pegasus, who some say is his brother.

Object of interest
Epsilon Equulei is a double star, of magnitudes 5·3 and 7·1, easily seen through small telescopes.

Eridanus the river

An exceptionally long constellation, meandering from the celestial equator, by the foot of Orion, to Hydrus in the deep south. In terms of area, Eridanus is the sixth largest constellation in the sky. Eridanus has been identified through the ages with many mythical and real rivers, including the Nile and Euphrates.

Objects of interest
Alpha Eridani (Achernar, end of the river) is a blue-white star of magnitude 0·5, 78 light years from us. It is the ninth-brightest star in the sky.
Epsilon Eridani, magnitude 3·7, is among the nearest stars to the Sun, being 10·7 light years away. It is slightly smaller and cooler than our Sun, and may have an invisible companion star or large planet.
Theta Eridani is a striking duo of blue-white stars, magnitudes 3·4 and 4·4, easily separated through small telescopes.
Omicron-2 Eridani (also known as 40 Eridani) is a remarkable triple star

containing the most easily observable white dwarf. Through small telescopes, Omicron-2 Eridani appears to be a wide double star, of magnitudes 4·5 and 9·5; the fainter component is the white dwarf. Telescope apertures of 75 millimetres (3 inches) and more show that the white dwarf has an 11th-magnitude red dwarf companion. This remarkable combination is well worth finding.
32 Eridani is a colourful double star to be seen through small telescopes. It consists of yellow and blue-green stars of magnitudes 5 and 6·3.

Fornax the furnace

A barren constellation of the southern skies, one of the introductions of Lacaille, who originally called it Fornax Chemica, the chemical furnace. The constellation's main point of interest is that it contains a dwarf elliptical galaxy known as 'the Fornax System', a member of our Local Group of galaxies. The Fornax dwarf galaxy lies 800 000 light years away from the Sun, quite close as galaxies go, but is so faint that it is visible only through large telescopes.

Gemini the twins

A major constellation of the northern hemisphere of the sky, and the third constellation of the Zodiac. The Sun passes through the constellation from late June to late July. Gemini represents the twin brothers Castor and Pollux, crewmen with Jason and the Argonauts; Castor and Pollux are depicted holding hands. Ancient mariners regarded the heavenly twins as symbols of good fortune, and this superstition is the origin of the polite oath 'By Jiminy' ('By Gemini'). One of the year's richest and brightest meteor

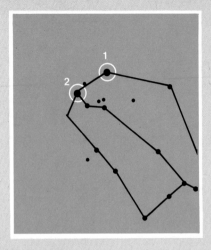

Gemini. **1**: Castor (Alpha Geminorum).
2: Pollux (Beta Geminorum).

showers, the Geminids, radiates from a point near Castor. A maximum of about 50 meteors an hour can be seen around 14 December each year.

Objects of interest
Alpha Geminorum (Castor) is an amazing six-star system. To the naked eye, Castor, which is 45 light years away, appears as a blue-white star of magnitude 1·6. A 60-millimetre (2·4-inch) aperture telescope splits Castor into two; the component stars orbit each other every 420 years. A ninth-magnitude red dwarf star visible farther away is also a member of the Castor system. Each of the three visible members of Castor is a spectroscopic binary, bringing the total of known stars in the system to six.
Beta Geminorum (Pollux) is the constellation's brightest star. It is a magnitude 1·2 orange giant, 35 light years away.
Delta Geminorum is a double star with components of widely unequal brightness (magnitudes 3·5 and 6·1,

colours cream and orange), requiring a 75-millimetre (3-inch) aperture telescope to separate them clearly.
M 35 (NGC 2168) is a large, bright star cluster just visible to the naked eye in clear skies and easily seen through binoculars. Small telescopes show its stars to be arranged in curving chains.
NGC 2392 is a planetary nebula appearing as a blue-green disc through telescopes of 100 millimetres (4 inches) or more aperture. Its central star is of ninth magnitude, the brightest of any planetary nebula.

Grus the crane

A constellation of the southern hemisphere of the sky, representing a long-necked water bird, introduced by Bayer. Its brightest star Alpha Gruis (Alnair) is of magnitude 2·2.

Objects of interest
Delta Gruis is a double star visible to the naked eye. It consists of two unrelated stars of magnitudes 4·0 and 4·3.
Mu Gruis is another duo of unrelated stars, magnitudes 4·9 and 5·2, also visible to the naked eye.

Hercules

The fifth-largest constellation in the sky, and a major figure of the north celestial hemisphere, although it does not contain any outstandingly bright stars. The constellation represents to us the well-known hero of Greek mythology who undertook 12 labours to gain release from the service of a Greek king. Various peoples throughout the ages have identified the constellation with their own heroes or gods, including the Sumerian superman, Gilgamesh. Hercules is usually depicted kneeling, with one foot on the head of Draco, the dragon. The constellation contains many double stars, as does neighbouring Bootes, and boasts the finest globular cluster in northern skies.

Objects of interest

Alpha Herculis (Ras Algethi, the kneeler's head) is a red supergiant star which varies erratically in brightness between third and fourth magnitudes. Small telescopes show it has a blue-green companion of magnitude 5·4.

Delta Herculis, magnitude 3·2, has a ninth-magnitude companion visible through small telescopes.

Rho Herculis can be resolved by small telescopes into components of magnitudes 4·5 and 5·5.

95 Herculis is a gold and silver duo visible through small telescopes. The two stars have magnitudes of 5·2 and 5·1 respectively.

M 13 (NGC 6205) is one of the most impressive globular clusters in the entire sky, visible as a misty patch to the naked eye in clear skies and easily found through binoculars. Small telescopes resolve individual stars in the cluster, showing a mottled appearance. M 13 lies 24 000 light years away from the Sun.

M 92 (NGC 6341) is a major globular cluster visible through binoculars, only slightly inferior to M 13.

Globular cluster M 13 in Hercules is the finest such cluster in northern skies.

Horologium
the pendulum clock

Another of the obscure southern constellations representing various mechanical devices, and intoduced in the 1750s by Lacaille. Its brightest star is only of magnitude 3·8. Horologium contains little to interest amateur astronomers.

Hydra the water snake

The largest constellation in the sky, representing a water snake guarding Crater, the cup, from Corvus, the crow, in punishment for the latter's neglect of its errand to bring water. But the constellation has also been depicted as a dragon, a role now exclusively filled by Draco.

The water snake's head lies just north of the celestial equator, on the borders of Cancer and Leo, and its body stretches over 100° to the edge of Lupus in the southern celestial hemisphere. For all its enormous size,

Hydra contains only one star of any prominence: Alpha Hydrae (Alphard, aptly known as the Solitary One), an orange giant of magnitude 2·2, which marks the water snake's heart.

Objects of interest
Epsilon Hydrae is a close but colourful pair of third- and seventh-magnitude stars to be seen through telescopes of 75 millimetres (3 inches), or more, aperture.
M 48 (NGC 2548) is a cluster, visible through binoculars, of 50 or so stars arranged in a triangular grouping.
M 83 (NGC 5236) is an eighth-magnitude spiral galaxy seen face-on, one of the galaxies of the southern sky most easily seen through small telescopes.
NGC 3242 is a ninth-magnitude planetary nebula visible through small telescopes as a blue-green disc of equivalent apparent size to the planet Jupiter.

M 83 is a spiral galaxy in Hydra and one of the most prominent galaxies of the southern celestial hemisphere.

128

Hydrus
the lesser water snake

An unimpressive constellation deep in the southern hemisphere of the sky, lying between the Magellanic Clouds. Hydrus was introduced by Bayer as a counterpart of the great water snake, Hydra, visible in northern skies. The brightest stars of Hydrus are of only third magnitude, and there is nothing at all remarkable within its boundaries.

Indus the Indian

A faint constellation far down in the southern sky, introduced by Bayer. It represents a North American Indian and contains no stars brighter than third magnitude.

Object of interest
Epsilon Indi is one of the closest stars to the Sun, lying 11·2 light years away. It is an orange dwarf, somewhat smaller and cooler than the Sun, and shines at magnitude 4·7.

Lacerta the lizard

An inconspicuous constellation, its brightest star being of the fourth magnitude, introduced by Hevelius to include the stars between Cygnus and Andromeda in the northern sky. Lacerta lies on the edge of the Milky Way, and is a good area for novae, three having occurred within its boundaries this century. A 14th-magnitude object called BL Lacertae, once thought to be a peculiar variable star, has turned out to be the prototype of a family of energetic galaxies related to quasars. These objects are now known as *BL Lac objects*, or sometimes as Lacertids.

Trails of meteors photographed during the great Leonid meteor storm of 1966.

Leo the lion

A major constellation of the northern celestial hemisphere, and one of the few constellations which looks at all like the object it is supposed to represent − in this case a crouching lion, perhaps the lion slain by Hercules. The sickle shape of stars which form the lion's head and mane is unmistakable. Leo is the fifth constellation of the Zodiac. The Sun passes through the constellation from mid-August to mid-September.

Leo contains numerous distant galaxies, only a few of which are within easy reach of amateur telescopes. Each year, the Leonid meteor shower radiates from a point near Gamma Leonis, reaching a maximum on 17 November. Usually no more than about 10 Leonid meteors per hour are visible, but on occasions sudden storms have occurred when meteors have appeared to fall from the sky like snowflakes. The last such Leonid meteor storm was seen from the United States in 1966. Alas, there seems no chance of a repeat performance of this spectacle in the near future.

Objects of interest

Alpha Leonis (Regulus, the royal one) is a blue-white star of magnitude 1·3, 84 light years away from us. Bin- oculars or small telescopes reveal a wide eighth-magnitude companion.

Gamma Leonis (Algieba, lion's mane) is an outstanding pair of golden stars of magnitudes 2·6 and 3·8 visible through telescopes of all sizes. Binoculars show an unrelated fifth-magnitude yellow star nearby.

M 65 and M 66 (NGC 3623 and NGC 3627) are a pair of ninth-magnitude spiral galaxies lying about 30 million light years away from us. They may be

M 66 is a spiral galaxy in Leo.

detected as elongated misty patches through large binoculars under clear conditions, but need telescopes of at least 100 millimetres (4 inches) aperture and low power to be seen well.

M 95 and M 96 (NGC 3351 and NGC 3368) are a pair of 10th-magnitude spiral galaxies seen face-on. They are about 30 million light years away, the same distance as M 65 and M 66 to which they are probably related. M 95 and M 96 appear as circular patches of light through small telescopes.

Leo Minor the lesser lion

A cub lion, lying between Leo and Ursa Major in the northern sky. Leo Minor was introduced by Hevelius. Its brightest stars are only of fourth magnitude, and there is nothing here to attract attention.

Lepus the hare

A constellation of the southern hemisphere of the sky, representing a hare hiding under the feet of its hunter,

M 95, a barred spiral galaxy in Leo, appears circular through small telescopes.

Orion. Some people associate the hare with the Moon, because the dark markings on the Moon's face resemble a hare with pointed ears. The constellation's brightest star, of magnitude 2·7, is called Arneb, the Arabic for hare.

Objects of interest

Gamma Leporis is an attractive, wide double star of yellow and orange components, magnitudes 3·8 and 6·4, separable through small telescopes or even binoculars.

M 79 (NGC 1904) is an eighth-magnitude globular cluster, not one of the most impressive to be seen through small telescopes. But near to it lies an interesting triple star observable through small telescopes, called Herschel 3752, with components of magnitudes six, seven and nine.

Libra the scales

The seventh constellation of the Zodiac, lying just south of the celestial equator. Libra originally represented the claws of the neighbouring scorpion, Scorpius, but during Roman times it became a separate constellation which is now represented as the scales of justice. The scales are frequently depicted being held in the hand of Astraea, goddess of justice, who in one legend is identified with neighbouring Virgo. The Sun passes through the constellation of Libra during November.

Objects of interest
Alpha Librae (Zubenelgenubi, the southern claw) is a magnitude 2·9 blue-white star with a wide companion of magnitude 5·3 which is visible through binoculars.
Delta Librae is an eclipsing binary star of similar type to Algol in Perseus. Delta Librae varies between magnitudes 4·8 and 5·9 every 2 days 8 hours.

Lupus the wolf

A constellation of the southern hemisphere of the sky, representing a wolf held in the clutches of Centaurus, the centaur. Although Lupus lies in a rich area of the Milky Way it is not very prominent, its brightest stars being of third magnitude.

Objects of interest
Eta Lupi is a double star with magnitudes of 3·6 and 7·7, visible through small telescopes.
Kappa Lupi is a duo of blue-white stars of magnitudes 4·1 and 6, easily seen through small telescopes.
NGC 5822 is a cluster, visible through binoculars, of over 100 stars.

Lynx the lynx

A faint constellation of the northern sky, filling a gap devoid of prominent stars between Ursa Major and Auriga. It was introduced by Hevelius, who chose the name Lynx because only the lynx-eyed would be able to see it! Its brightest star is of magnitude 3·3, but among its fainter members are several noted double and multiple stars.

Object of interest
12 Lyncis is an attractive triple star, worth taking the trouble to find. Small telescopes show it as a double star of magnitudes 4·9 and 8·5, but from apertures of 75 millimetres (3 inches) and over, the brighter star has two components of magnitudes 5·4 and 6·0.

Lyra the lyre

A small but distinctive constellation in the northern hemisphere of the sky, lying under the wing of Cygnus. In Greek mythology, Lyra represents the stringed instrument, the lyre, which Orpheus played, although the constellation has also been represented as an eagle or vulture. Lyra's brightest star, Vega, forms one corner of the Summer Triangle of stars that is completed by Deneb in Cygnus and Altair in Aquila. Vega will become the Pole Star in about 12 000 years as a result of the movement, known as precession, of the Earth's North Pole.

Lyra is the radiant point of two meteor showers each year. The first, the April Lyrids, reach a maximum of about 20 meteors per hour on 21 or 22 April. The June Lyrids are less abundant, peaking at about 8 meteors per hour on 16 June each year.

Objects of interest
Alpha Lyrae (Vega, the Arabic name for the constellation) is the fifth-brightest star in the sky. It is exactly of magnitude 0, and is a brilliant blue-white. Vega lies 26 light years from us, which is relatively close.

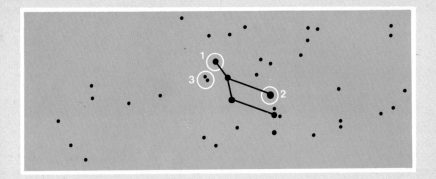

Above: Lyra, showing main stars of interest. **1**: Alpha Lyrae (Vega). **2**: Beta Lyrae. **3**: Epsilon Lyrae.

Beta Lyrae (Sheliak) is both a double and a variable star. Small telescopes show it to be an attractive pair of yellow and blue stars. The brighter star (the yellow one) is actually an eclipsing binary which varies between magnitudes 3·4 and 4·3 every 12 days 22 hours.

Epsilon Lyrae is the finest quadruple star in the sky; it is commonly termed the 'double double'. Binoculars, or even keen eyesight, show it as a double, of magnitudes 4·5 and 4·7. But telescopes of 75 to 100 millimetres (3 to 4 inches) aperture and high magnification reveal that each double star is itself a close double.

M 57 (NGC 6720) is a well-known planetary nebula, commonly termed the Ring Nebula. It is visible as an elliptical misty patch through small

Below: Ring Nebula is visible as an elliptical patch through small telescopes.

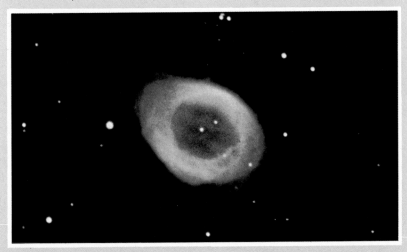

telescopes midway between Beta and Gamma Lyrae, but is far less impressive than its appearance in long-exposure photographs.

Mensa the table mountain

A constellation near the south celestial pole and one of the introductions of Lacaille who named it in honour of Table Mountain in South Africa. From this mountain, he made his observations of the southern skies in the 1750s.

Mensa contains part of the Large Magellanic Cloud, most of which lies in neighbouring Doradus. Otherwise, the constellation is almost totally barren, with no star brighter than fifth magnitude.

Microscopium
the microscope

Another of Lacaille's obscure constellations of the southern hemisphere, this one representing a microscope. Its brightest stars are of only fifth magnitude, and the constellation acts as nothing more than a filler between the better-known figures of Crux and Sagittarius.

Monoceros the unicorn

An interesting constellation of the equatorial region of the sky, between Orion and Canis Minor. Monoceros represents the mythical single-horned animal, the unicorn. The constellation's description is usually attributed to the German mathematician Jakob Bartsch in 1624, although its origin probably goes back much further than that. Monoceros is faint, with no star brighter than fourth magnitude, but it boasts instead a host of fascinating

double stars, clusters, and nebulae, only a few of which can be mentioned here.

Objects of interest
Beta Monocerotis is a celebrated triple star to be seen with small telescopes. Its three members, all white, are of magnitudes 4·7, 5·2, and 5·6, forming a narrow triangle.
Epsilon Monocerotis is a duo of yellow and blue stars of magnitudes 4·5 and 6·5, easily seen through small telescopes.
M 50 (NGC 2323) is a cluster, visible through binoculars, of about 100 stars. Telescopes reveal a red star near the centre.
NGC 2244 is a cluster, visible through binoculars, of about 15 stars, including the sixth-magnitude yellow giant 12 Monocerotis. The cluster has recently formed from a surrounding cloud of gas, known as the Rosette Nebula because of its beautiful flower-like appearance on long-exposure photographs. Unfortunately, the Rosette Nebula itself is too faint to show as anything more than a smudge through amateur telescopes.
NGC 2264 is a large, scattered cluster of about 20 main stars, including the fifth-magnitude S Monocerotis, which is slightly variable. It is visible through binoculars. Long-exposure photographs show that the cluster is embedded in a glowing nebula. The nebula includes a dark, conical lane which gives it the name of 'the Cone Nebula'.

Musca the fly

A small and faint constellation of the deep southern skies, introduced by Bayer under the name of Apis, the

Above, right: The Rosette Nebula which is associated with a star cluster.
Right: The dark Cone Nebula.

bee, which other astronomers subsequently changed. The tip of the dark Coalsack Nebula intrudes into Musca from neighbouring Crux, but otherwise the constellation has little of interest to users of small telescopes.

Norma the level

A small, faint constellation of southern skies representing a surveyor's level, introduced by Lacaille. Norma has no stars labelled Alpha or Beta because of changes in the constellation's boundaries, which have resulted in those stars being transferred under new names to surrounding constellations. Thus, the brightest star left in Norma is only of fourth magnitude. The constellation lies in the Milky Way, but there is little to attract the amateur observer.

Octans the octant

A faint constellation containing the south pole of the sky, and introduced by Lacaille. As with so many of Lacaille's introductions, the constellation itself is totally unremarkable. Octans represents an instrument known as the octant, a forerunner of the modern sextant.

Object of interest
Sigma Octantis is the nearest star to the south celestial pole (lying about one degree from the true pole position) which is visible to the naked eye. It is only of magnitude 5·5, far less impressive than the equivalent Polaris of northern skies.

Ophiuchus the serpent holder

A large, though not particularly prominent constellation, straddling the celestial equator. Ophiuchus is visualized as a man holding a serpent (the constellation Serpens). Ophiuchus is

S-shaped dark nebula silhouetted against Milky Way star fields in Ophiuchus.

identified with Aesculapius, a mythical Greek healer who was ship's doctor to Jason and his crew on the ship Argo, and who was said to be an ancestor of the great Greek physician Hippocrates. Although Ophiuchus is not a zodiacal constellation, the Sun passes through it from late November to mid December.

Ophiuchus lies in the Milky Way, and contains rich star fields and numerous globular clusters, two of which are prominent. Several interesting dark nebulae appear silhouetted against the bright Milky Way star fields in this region. The brightest star in Ophiuchus, Alpha Ophiuchi (called Ras Alhague, head of the serpent charmer), is of second magnitude. One of the constellation's most interesting stars is invisible to the naked eye: ninth-magnitude Barnard's Star, a red dwarf which is the second-closest star to the Sun, being only 6 light years away.

Orion's belt is a line of three stars. His sword is marked by the Orion Nebula.

Objects of interest
70 Ophiuchi is a showpiece double star, 17 light years away. It consists of a close yellow and orange duo, of magnitudes 4·3 and 6·0, which require a 100-millimetre (4-inch) aperture and high magnification to separate them.
M10 (NGC 6254) is a seventh-magnitude globular cluster forming a neat pair with M12 some 3·5° away, and visible through binoculars and small telescopes.
M12 (NGC 6218) is an eighth-magnitude globular cluster, larger and more loosely scattered than M10, visible through binoculars or small telescopes.

Orion the hunter

A glorious constellation, set squarely on the celestial equator, and among the most distinctive figures of the entire sky. Orion is depicted as a great hunter or warrior, brandishing a club in one hand and raising his shield towards the charging bull, Taurus. Orion's two brightest stars, Rigel and Betelgeuse, mark the hunter's left leg and right shoulder respectively. His belt is marked by a line of three stars. Below the belt hangs his sword, where the famous Orion Nebula lies.

Many peoples have identified this constellation with their own national gods and heroes. The British author J. R. R. Tolkien tells us that the Hobbit folk of his fictional Middle Earth knew the constellation as Menelvagor, the Swordsman of the Sky. According to popular Greek mythology, Orion was stung to death by a scorpion (represented by the constellation Scorpius). Orion is opposite to the scorpion in the sky, so that as the scorpion rises Orion sets. An annual meteor shower, the Orionids, radiates from a point near the border with Scorpius. Up to 30 Orionid meteors per hour can be seen on 21 October each year.

Objects of interest

Alpha Orionis (Betelgeuse, the left shoulder of Orion) is a supergiant red star, so big that it could contain the orbit of the planet Mars. Betelgeuse is too large to be stable and fluctuates irregularly in size, varying in brightness between magnitudes 0·4 and 1·3 as it does so. Betelgeuse is an estimated 650 light years away.

Beta Orionis (Rigel, giant's leg) is a blue-white supergiant star of magnitude 0·1, the brightest star in Orion and the sixth-brightest star in the entire sky. Its estimated distance is 850 light years. Rigel has a seventh-magnitude companion star, difficult to see through telescopes of less than 150 millimetres (6 inches) aperture

because of the primary's glare, particularly in unsteady air.

Zeta Orionis is a close double star of magnitudes 2·0 and 4·2, requiring telescope apertures of 75 millimetres (3 inches) and above to resolve them.

Eta Orionis is another close double, of magnitudes 3·7 and 5·1, visible through telescopes of at least 100 millimetres (4 inches) aperture.

Theta-1 Orionis is the name of a famous quadruple star at the heart of the Orion Nebula. Its four components, of magnitudes 5·4, 6·8, 6·9 and 7·9, form a shape known as the Trapezium and can easily be separated through small telescopes. The light from these stars illuminates the Orion Nebula.

Theta-2 Orionis, which lies near Theta-1 Orionis, is a wide double, magnitudes 5·2 and 6·5.

Horsehead Nebula in Orion is a dark dust cloud of distinctive shape, silhouetted against an area of glowing gas.

Orion. **1**: Alpha Orionis (Betelgeuse).
2: Beta Orionis (Rigel).

Iota Orionis is a double star at the southern edge of the Orion Nebula, separable through small telescopes into components of magnitudes 2·9 and 7·4.
Lambda Orionis is a magnitude 3·7 star with a close, magnitude 5·6 companion visible through small telescopes at high magnification.
Sigma Orionis appears through telescopes of 60 millimetres (2·4 inches) aperture as a colourful triple star of magnitudes 3·8 (blue-white in colour), 6·5 (bluish) and 7·5 (reddish). Apertures of 150 millimetres (6 inches) reveal a 10th-magnitude star close to the primary, thereby making this a striking quadruple group. Also nearby is a faint triple star, Struve 761, consisting of eighth- and ninth-magnitude stars in a triangle.
M 42 (NGC 1976), the Orion Nebula, is one of the treasures of the sky. It is a glowing cloud of gas about 1300 light years away and at least 10 light years in diameter, part of an area of star-formation in our Galaxy that encompasses the whole constellation of Orion. The Orion Nebula, visible as a misty patch to the naked eye, is a magnificent sight through all instruments from binoculars upwards, showing delicate loops of greenish gas.
M 43 (NGC 1982) is a smaller, rounded nebulosity just north of the Orion Nebula, and centred on a ninth-magnitude star. Long-exposure photographs show M 43 to be part of the same cloud as M 42.

Pavo the peacock

A constellation of the southern sky, introduced by Bayer. Pavo represents a peacock, a bird said to be a symbol of immortality. The peacock's starry tail made it sacred to the goddess Juno, Queen of the Heavens. In another story, the peacock represents Argos, builder of Jason's ship the Argo, and who subsequently became immortal. The constellation's brightest star, Alpha Pavonis, magnitude 2·1, is actually called Peacock.

Objects of interest
Xi Pavonis is a colourful double star consisting of red and white components, magnitudes 4·3 and 8·6, and visible through small telescopes.
NGC 6752 is a seventh-magnitude globular cluster, visible through binoculars, which is rated among the finest such clusters in the heavens.

Pegasus the winged horse

Pegasus represents the mythical winged horse that was born from the fearsome Medusa's blood that fell into the ocean after Medusa was decapitated by Perseus. A more modern legend depicts Pegasus as the steed of Perseus during his rescue of Andromeda, but ancient mythology does not support this interpretation.

The constellation, which lies just north of the celestial equator, is the seventh largest in the sky, but contains few outstanding objects. Its distinguishing feature is the famous Square, one corner of which is marked by the star Alpha Andromedae, 'borrowed' from the neighbouring constellation of Andromeda. Curiously, the interior of the great Square of Pegasus is almost entirely devoid of stars visible to the naked eye — unusual for such a large area of sky.

Objects of interest
Beta Pegasi (Scheat, shoulder) is a red giant variable star which fluctuates between second and third magnitude.
Epsilon Pegasi (Enif, the nose) is a yellow star of magnitude 2·5 with a wide ninth-magnitude companion which is visible through binoculars.

Below: M 15 is a globular cluster in Pegasus, visible through binoculars.

M 15 (NGC 7078) is a sixth-magnitude globular cluster, one of the finest in northern skies. Binoculars and small telescopes show it as a misty patch in an attractive field. Telescopes of about 150 millimetres (6 inches) aperture resolve its outer regions into individual stars.

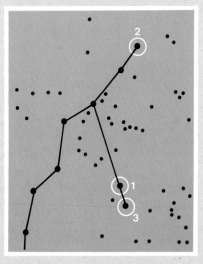

Above: Perseus. **1**: Beta Persei (Algol). **2**: Eta Persei. **3**: Rho Persei.

Perseus

A constellation of northern skies, representing a hero of Greek mythology who rescued Andromeda from being eaten alive by the sea monster, Cetus. Perseus is depicted holding in his hand the severed head of Medusa, the Gorgon, whose evil glance could turn people to stone.

Perseus lies in a rich region of the Milky Way, and contains several celebrated clusters and individual stars, including the noted variable star Algol (which marks the Gorgon's evil eye).

Showpiece 'double cluster' in Perseus.

The constellation's brightest star, Alpha Persei (also known as Algenib or Mirfak), of magnitude 1·9, lies in a particularly star-studded region. Perseus is the radiant of the year's best-known meteor shower, the Perseids, which appears every August. Up to 60 bright meteors per hour can be seen around 12 and 13 August radiating from a point near Gamma Persei.

Objects of interest
Beta Persei (Algol, the demon) is the classic example of an eclipsing variable star, in which one star is temporarily eclipsed by a darker companion star. Algol is eclipsed by its companion every 2 days 21 hours when its brightness falls from magnitude 2·2 to 3·5. The eclipses last 10 hours.
Eta Persei is a colourful double star consisting of orange and blue components of magnitudes 3·9 and 8·6,

and visible through small telescopes.
Rho Persei is a red giant that varies somewhat erratically between magnitudes 3·3 and 4·0 every five or six weeks.
M 34 (NGC 1039) is a scattered cluster, visible through binoculars, of about 80 stars.
NGC 869 and NGC 884, the famous 'double cluster', are twin star clusters visible to the naked eye as fuzzy patches, like brighter regions of the Milky Way, each covering the same area of sky as the full Moon. They are so bright that they have been entered on star maps under the names h and Chi Persei. Because of their large size they are best seen through binoculars or small, wide-angle telescopes. The double cluster is a showpiece visible through all apertures.

Phoenix the phoenix

A constellation of the southern skies, introduced by Bayer to represent the mythical bird that symbolizes immortality. Its brightest star, Alpha Phoenicis, is of magnitude 2·4.

Objects of interest
Beta Phoenicis is a close pair of stars of magnitude 4, requiring telescopes of 100 millimetres (4 inches) aperture to distinguish them.
Zeta Phoenicis is a fourth-magnitude star with an eighth-magnitude companion visible through small telescopes.

Pictor the painter's easel

This small and faint constellation was originally introduced in the 1750s by de Lacaille under the full title Equuleus Pictoris, which has since been shortened. It is intended to represent a painter's easel, for obscure reasons. Pictor contains nothing to attract amateur observers.

Pisces the fishes

The twelfth constellation of the Zodiac, lying in the equatorial region of the sky. The Sun passes through the constellation from mid-March to mid-April. Pisces is visualized as two fishes, with their tails tied together by a cord; the connecting knot is marked by the star Alpha Piscium. According to legend, Venus and her son Cupid turned into fishes — or, in an alternative version, they were carried away by two fishes — to escape the monster Typhon. Pisces is faint, and not easy to identify.

Object of interest
Alpha Piscium (Al Rischa, the cord) is a close duo of blue-white stars, magnitudes 4·3 and 5·2, needing at least 75 millimetres (3 inches) aperture and high magnification to separate them.

Piscis Austrinus
the southern fish

A southern hemisphere constellation, also known as Piscis Australis, representing a fish drinking the flow of water from the urn of Aquarius. Legend has it that this fish is the parent of the twin fishes of Pisces. One legend even equates Piscis Austrinus with the Egyptian fish god Oannes.

The constellation's brightest star, Alpha Piscis Austrini, known as Fomalhaut from the Arabic for fish's mouth, is of magnitude 1·2. Apart from this first-magnitude star, Piscis Austrinus contains no prominent objects.

Puppis the stern

The largest part of the former giant constellation of Argo Navis, the ship of the Argonauts, which was broken up into four smaller constellations by Lacaille. Puppis, which represents the stern or poop of the ship, lies in a rich Milky Way area, and contains many objects of note.

Objects of interest
Zeta Puppis (Naos, the ship), the brightest star in the constellation, is one of the most intensely hot and luminous stars known. It appears to be magnitude 2·2, and lies at an estimated distance of over 2000 light years. To appear so bright over such a vast distance, Zeta Puppis must give out as much light as 60 000 Suns.
Kappa Puppis is a blue-white duo of

nearly identical stars, magnitudes 4·5 and 4·6, resolved by small telescopes. **L Puppis** consists of two unrelated stars. L_1 is of fifth magnitude. L_2 is a red giant that varies between third and sixth magnitude every five months or so.

M 47 (NGC 2422) is the brightest of several clusters in Puppis, consisting of about 50 stars as bright as sixth magnitude, just visible to the naked eye and easily visible through binoculars.

M 46 (NGC 2437) is another cluster, containing more but fainter stars, and lies about 1·5° away from M 47.

NGC 2477 is a sixth-magnitude cluster, visible through binoculars, consisting of about 300 faint stars densely packed.

Pyxis the compass

An unimportant constellation of the southern skies, representing the compass of the ship Argo Navis. Lacaille described the constellation under the name Pyxis Nautica, the mariner's compass, which has since been shortened. Pyxis is the smallest and faintest of the four constellations which go to make up the ship Argo (the other parts being Carina, Puppis, and Vela). Its brightest stars are of fourth magnitude.

Reticulum the net

Another of the dim constellations introduced by Lacaille. Reticulum commemorates an instrument known as the reticle, used to measure star positions. Perhaps the constellation's most celebrated star is Zeta Reticuli, a wide pair of fifth-magnitude stars both similar to the Sun, lying 30 light years away from it, and visible through binoculars.

Sagitta the arrow

The third smallest constellation of the sky, lying north of Aquila in the northern celestial hemisphere. It represents an arrow, which various legends associate with various mythical archers. Perhaps the most fitting story says it was shot by Hercules towards the birds Cygnus and Aquila, between which it is passing. Sagitta lies in a dense part of the Milky Way, and like its neighbours Delphinus and Vulpecula it is a good area for the occurrence of novae. The stars of Sagitta are of fourth magnitude or less.

Sagittarius the archer

One of the richest constellations, for it contains the centre of our Galaxy; consequently the Milky Way star fields are particularly dense in this direction, including numerous nebulae and star clusters. The French astronomer Messier catalogued 15 objects within its boundaries, more than in any other constellation.

Sagittarius lies in the southern hemisphere of the sky, and represents the mythical creature known as a centaur. This is a very different centaur from the benevolent character represented by Centaurus. Sagittarius is a warlike creature, with a raised bow aimed at the heart of neighbouring Scorpius, the scorpion. Sagittarius is the ninth constellation of the Zodiac; the Sun passes through it from mid-December to mid-January. The exact centre of our Galaxy is marked by a radio source known as Sagittarius A, lying near the borders with Scorpius and Ophiuchus.

Objects of interest
M 8 (NGC 6523), the Lagoon Nebula,

144

Left: Lagoon Nebula, M 8, in Sagittarius.

is a gas cloud visible as a fifth-magnitude misty patch to the naked eye, covering twice the apparent area of the full Moon. Within the nebula is a cluster of about 25 stars of seventh magnitude and less, recently formed from the surrounding gas. Binoculars or small telescopes show the cluster and the enveloping nebula, although the full glory of M 8 becomes apparent only on long-exposure photographs.

M 17 (NGC 6618), the Omega Nebula, is a glowing gas cloud visible under good conditions through binoculars or small telescopes as an elongated smudge. Its true horseshoe-shape is brought out in long-exposure photographs.

M 22 (NGC 6656) is a sixth-magnitude globular cluster, rated as one of the finest such clusters in the sky. It is visible through binoculars and is noticeably elliptical in outline. Its outer regions can be resolved into stars by telescopes of 75 millimetres (3 inches) aperture.

M 23 (NGC 6494) is a large cluster of 100 or more stars of ninth magnitude and less, visible through binoculars or small telescopes.

Scorpius the scorpion

A brilliant constellation in the southern hemisphere of the sky, representing a scorpion with its curved tail raised to strike. This is said to be the scorpion whose sting killed Orion. The sting of the scorpion is marked by the star Lambda Scorpii, magnitude 1·6, which is also known as Shaula, a name that comes from the Arabic for 'sting'. The scorpion's heart is marked by the red giant Antares.

Omega Nebula, M 17, shows a complex shape on long-exposure photographs.

Rich Milky Way star fields in Scorpius, looking towards the centre of the Galaxy.

Scorpius is the eighth constellation of the Zodiac; the Sun passes briefly through the constellation during the last week of November. Scorpius contains rich Milky Way star fields towards the centre of our Galaxy, and has many sights for observers.

Objects of interest
Alpha Scorpii (Antares, rival of Mars) is a red supergiant so-named because its colour rivals that of the red planet Mars. Antares is several hundred times the diameter of the Sun — so large that it is unstable. It pulsates irregularly in size, varying in brightness as it does so between magnitudes 0·9 and 1·1. Antares has a sixth-magnitude blue companion, requiring at least 75 millimetres (3 inches) aperture to be visible in the primary's glare.
Beta Scorpii is a double star, con-
sisting of blue-white stars of magnitudes 2·9 and 5·1, easily visible through small telescopes.
Nu Scorpii is a quadruple star, similar to Lyra's so-called 'double double'. Small telescopes show Nu Scorpii as a wide pair of fourth- and sixth-magnitude stars. The fainter star is split again through telescope apertures of 75 millimetres (3 inches) or more, while the brighter star requires at least 150 millimetres aperture to separate the components.
Xi Scorpii is a double star with yellow and orange components of magnitudes 4·2 and 7·2, to be seen through small telescopes. Also visible in the same telescopic field is a fainter but wider double, called Struve 1999,

146

which is related to the main pair, thereby making this a contrasting multiple system.

M 4 (NGC 6121) is a large seventh-magnitude globular cluster lying near Antares, and visible through binoculars and small telescopes.

M 6 (NGC 6405) is a star cluster, consisting of about 50 main stars of sixth magnitude or less, but visible through binoculars.

M 7 (NGC 6475) is a large and bright star cluster visible to the naked eye, and easily resolved into individual

Distinctive shape of the constellation of Scorpius. Alpha Scorpii (Antares) is circled; it marks the scorpion's heart.

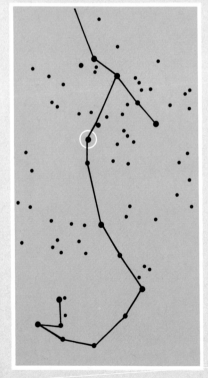

stars through binoculars and small telescopes.

NGC 6231 is a bright cluster whose main stars, as seen through binoculars, form a group like a mini Pleiades (see page 149).

Sculptor the sculptor

Another faint constellation of the southern skies introduced by Lacaille, and containing no stars brighter than fourth magnitude. The constellation is intended to represent a sculptor's workshop. Although the stars of Sculptor are of no particular interest, the constellation does contain numerous distant galaxies, all unfortunately beyond the range of small amateur instruments. Perhaps the most interesting galaxy in Sculptor is a dwarf elliptical member of our own Local Group, so faint that it can be detected only on long-exposure photographs.

Scutum the shield

A small constellation in rich Milky Way star fields just south of the celestial equator. The constellation was introduced by Hevelius under the title Scutum Sobieskii (Sobieski's shield), in honour of his patron King John Sobieskii. Scutum, as it is now known, is the fifth-smallest constellation in the sky, and its brightest star is only of fourth magnitude.

Object of interest

M 11 (NGC 6705) is a famous and beautiful star cluster, known commonly as 'the Wild Duck Cluster' because its fan shape resembles a group of ducks in flight. M 11 is visible as a misty patch through binoculars, but telescopes resolve it into a sparkling field of individual stars, with a brighter orange star near the apex.

Eagle Nebula, M 16, in Serpens.

Serpens the serpent

This constellation is split into two entirely separate parts! Serpens represents a snake entwined around the body of Ophiuchus, the serpent bearer. The head of the snake is represented by the part called Serpens Caput; the snake's tail is formed by Serpens Cauda, which is the smaller and fainter half. Both parts of Serpens lie in the equatorial region of the sky.

Objects of interest
Delta Serpentis is a close duo of white stars, magnitudes 4·2 and 5·2, separated through telescope apertures of 60 millimetres or more with high magnification.
Theta Serpentis is a wide double of magnitudes 4·5 and 5·4, separable through good binoculars and an object easily seen through small telescopes.

M 5 (NGC 5904) is a sixth-magnitude globular cluster, visible through binoculars and small telescopes, and rated among the finest in the northern sky. Apertures of 100 millimetres (4 inches), or more, show chains of stars radiating from its bright central core.
M 16 (NGC 6611) is a scattered cluster, visible through binoculars, of stars of eighth magnitude or less. Long-exposure photographs show the cluster to be surrounded by a glowing gas cloud known as 'the Eagle Nebula'.

Sextans the sextant

An unremarkable constellation, lying in the equatorial region of the sky, whose brightest star is magnitude 4·5. Sextans was introduced by Hevelius to commemorate the sextant he used for measuring star positions.

Taurus the bull

A large and prominent constellation, extending northwards from the celestial equator. Taurus represents the head of a bull, seen snorting and charging at neighbouring Orion. The bull's glinting eye is represented by the red star Aldebaran, while the tips of his horns are marked by Beta and Zeta Tauri. The star Beta Tauri, incidentally, is shared with the constellation Auriga. Taurus is the second constellation of the Zodiac, through which the Sun passes from mid May to late June.

Taurus contains two of the sky's most famous star clusters: the large, scattered groups known as the Hyades and Pleiades. The Taurid meteors radiate from a point near Epsilon Tauri, reaching a maximum of about 12 meteors per hour on 8 November each year.

Objects of interest
Alpha Tauri (Aldebaran) is an orange giant star, of magnitude 0·9, lying about 65 light years from us. Although it appears to be part of the Hyades cluster, it is in fact much closer and is superimposed on them by chance.
M1 (NGC 1952), the Crab Nebula, is the remains of a star which Oriental astronomers saw explode as a supernova in AD 1054. All that is left is an expanding shell of gas surrounding the faint core of the shattered star. In 1968, astronomers discovered that this remnant core is a pulsar. Visually the Crab Nebula appears as an elliptical or slightly S-shaped white glow of ninth magnitude, visible through 75- to 100-millimetre (3- to 4-inch) aperture telescopes under good conditions. The nebula gets its name from its supposed resemblance to a crab with pincers.

The Pleiades (M 45) is a brilliant cluster of stars easily visible to the naked eye. The brightest star of the Pleiades, called Eta Tauri or Alcyone, is of third magnitude. The group is popularly known as the Seven Sisters, but as many as nine stars can be resolved by keen eyesight; binoculars bring dozens more stars into view. At least 200 stars are believed to belong to the cluster. Long-exposure photographs show the Pleiades to be enveloped in a hazy mist, the remains of the cloud from which the stars formed within the past few million years. The Pleiades lie 415 light years away, about 2·5 times the distance of the Hyades.
The Hyades is a very large, V-shaped cluster marking the head of the bull. Its

Location of the Hyades and Pleiades star clusters in Taurus with (*bottom*) names of the main stars in the Pleiades.

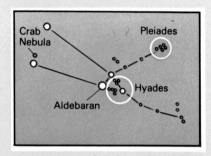

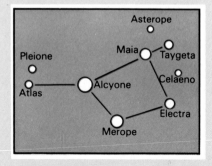

brightest stars are of magnitude 3·5
and as many as 24 of the Hyades stars
are visible to the naked eye under good
conditions. Hundreds more members
exist within the range of telescopes.

The brightest star in the Hyades,
Theta Tauri, is a double of magnitudes
3·6 and 4·0, visible through binoculars
or even to the naked eye. (The brilliant
star Aldebaran is not a member of the
Hyades, but is instead an unrelated
foreground object.) The Hyades lie
150 light years away.

Hyades and Pleiades star clusters in
Taurus are easy objects for observation
through binoculars, or for photography.

Telescopium the telescope

One of the many insignificant constellations of the southern hemisphere
described by Lacaille. Its brightest
stars are of no more than fourth magnitude, and Telescopium is an un-
worthy constellation to commemorate
the most important of astronomical
instruments, the telescope.

Triangulum the triangle

A small northern-hemisphere constellation, named after the distinctive

M 33 is a large but faint spiral galaxy in our Local Group, visible with binoculars as a misty patch in Triangulum.

shape formed by its three main stars.

Object of interest
M 33 (NGC 598) is a spiral galaxy in our own Local Group, lying about 2 million light years away, similar to the distance of the Andromeda Galaxy. M 33 is the third largest galaxy in the Local Group, after the Andromeda Galaxy and our own Milky Way. M 33 is presented to us almost face-on. It is large, covering the same area of sky as the full Moon, but it is very faint. It is best seen on a dark night through binoculars or a low-power telescope to enhance the contrast.

Triangulum Australe
the southern triangle

The sixth smallest constellation in the sky, whose name is self-explanatory. It was introduced by Bayer. The stars of Triangulum Australe are brighter than those of its northern counterpart, but the constellation contains no objects of particular note.

Tucana the toucan

A constellation of the far southern sky, introduced by Bayer and representing a large-beaked tropical bird. Its stars are not prominent, but it is of importance because it contains a major globular cluster and also the smaller of the two satellite galaxies that accompany the Milky Way.

Objects of interest
Beta Tucanae is a multiple star consisting of a duo of similar blue-white stars of magnitude 4·5, with a fainter fifth-magnitude star farther away. Beta Tucanae is evident as a multiple through binoculars and telescopes.
47 Tucanae is one of the most glorious globular clusters in the sky, second only in size and brightness to Omega Centauri. It is easily visible to the naked eye as a misty patch, and is so prominent that it was catalogued as

Small Magellanic Cloud in Tucana is a satellite galaxy of the Milky Way.

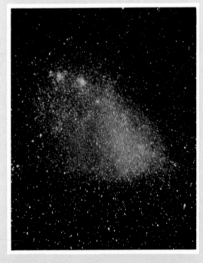

a star. Binoculars show it clearly, and telescopes of 100 millimetres (4 inches) aperture reveal individual stars in the cluster.
Small Magellanic Cloud is an irregularly shaped mini-galaxy about 160 000 light years away, containing as many as 1000 million stars, about one-tenth the number of the Large Magellanic Cloud in Dorado. To the naked eye, the Small Magellanic Cloud appears like a detached part of the Milky Way. Binoculars and telescopes reveal bright nebulae, clusters, and individual stars in the cloud.

Ursa Major the great bear

Probably the most familiar constellation of all, supposedly representing a bear, although most people know the shape formed by its seven brightest stars as 'the Plough' or 'Big Dipper'. Ursa Major is the third largest constellation, and lies in the northern hemisphere of the sky, next to Bootes, who is sometimes visualized as driving the bear around the pole. Two stars of the bowl of the dipper, known as Dubhe and Merak, form the so-called Pointers, since the continuation of a line drawn between them would point towards Polaris, the Pole Star. Ursa Major contains several interesting galaxies, only a few of which are within easy range of amateur telescopes.

Objects of interest
Zeta Ursae Majoris (Mizar) is a complex multiple star. Keen eyesight, or binoculars, show that Mizar, of magnitude 2·4, has a magnitude 4·0 companion, Alcor. Small telescopes show another fourth-magnitude star closer to Mizar. Studies have revealed that all of these stars are also spectroscopic binaries.
Xi Ursae Majoris is a duo of yellow stars of magnitudes 4·4 and 4·8, which

M 81 is a beautiful spiral galaxy in Ursa Major, visible through small telescopes.

orbit each other every 60 years. At their widest separation in 1975 they could be separated through small telescopes, but apertures of 150 millimetres (6 inches) will be needed to separate them when they are at their closest together in 1992.

M 81 (NGC 3031) and **M 82** (NGC 3034) form a contrasting pair of galaxies visible in the same telescopic field of view. M 81 is a beautiful face-on spiral of eighth magnitude, while M 82, half a degree away, is a ninth-magnitude bar-shaped galaxy which astronomers think may be exploding.

Ursa Minor the lesser bear

A constellation at the north pole of the sky. Its brightest star, Polaris, is the northern Pole Star. Ursa Minor represents a bear, a smaller companion of Ursa Major, although it is also known as 'the Little Dipper' because its seven main stars form a saucepan or ladle shape similar to that of the Big Dipper. The stars Beta Ursae Minoris (Kochab) and Gamma Ursae Minoris

(Pherkad) are sometimes termed 'the Guardians of the Pole'.

Object of interest
Alpha Ursae Minoris (Polaris or Cynosura) lies about one degree away from the true north pole of the sky. It is both a double and a variable star. Telescopes of 75 millimetres (3 inches) aperture show that Polaris has a wide ninth-magnitude companion star. Polaris is also the brightest Cepheid-type variable. It fluctuates every four days between magnitude 2·1 and 2·2, a change which is imperceptible to the naked eye.

Vela the sails

Part of the former giant southern-hemisphere constellation of Argo Navis, which was dismembered into four by Lacaille in the 1750s. Vela, being only a part of this once larger group, has no stars labelled Alpha or Beta. The stars Kappa and Delta Velorum, plus Iota and Epsilon Carinae, form the so-called 'false cross', which is occasionally mistaken for the true Southern Cross.

The Milky Way is particularly interesting in this area; long-exposure photographs reveal a large gas 'bubble' known as the Gum Nebula after the Australian radio astronomer Colin S. Gum who discovered it. This nebula is believed to be the remains of a supernova, presumably the event which gave rise to the Vela pulsar, the third fastest pulsar known and only the second pulsar ever seen visually; at magnitude 24, it is the faintest object ever detected optically.

Objects of interest
Gamma Velorum is a multiple star to be seen through binoculars and small telescopes. Binoculars show it to be a blue-white pair of magnitudes 2·2 and 4·8. The brighter star is the brightest Wolf-Rayet type of star, a class of exceptionally hot and luminous stars. Small telescopes show two wider companions, of ninth and tenth magnitude.
NGC 2547 is a cluster, visible through binoculars, of stars of seventh magnitude or less.

M 87, a giant elliptical galaxy in Virgo, is also known as the radio source Virgo A.

Virgo the virgin

The second largest constellation in the sky, and the sixth constellation of the Zodiac, through which the Sun passes from mid-September to early November. Virgo is visualized in some legends as a maiden holding an ear of wheat, and is thus considered to be a symbol of the harvest. The ear of wheat is represented by the constellation's brightest star, Spica (whose name means 'ear of wheat')., of magnitude one. Virgo is also seen as Astraea, goddess of justice, holding aloft the scales of justice (the neighbouring constellation of Libra).

Virgo contains a major cluster of galaxies 40 million light years away, the cluster extending over the border into Coma Berenices. The most prominent of these galaxies are mentioned below. Virgo also contains the brightest quasar, 3C 273, which appears optically as a 13th-magnitude star.

Objects of interest
Gamma Virginis (Porrima, named after a goddess of prophecy) is an outstanding double star to be seen through small telescopes and consists of twin yellow-white stars of magnitude 3·6.
M 49 (NGC 4472) is a ninth-magnitude elliptical galaxy visible as a rounded smudge through telescope apertures of 75 millimetres (3 inches) or more.
M 60 (NGC 4649) is another ninth-magnitude elliptical galaxy requiring telescope apertures of at least 75 millimetres (3 inches).
M 84 (NGC 4374) and **M 86**

(NGC 4406) are a pair of ninth-magnitude elliptical galaxies visible in the same telescopic field of view at the heart of the Virgo cluster.

M 87 (NGC 4486) is a famous elliptical galaxy which is also a radio and X-ray source. Through small telescopes it is visible as a rounded 10th-magnitude patch. Long-exposure photographs show a jet of matter apparently being ejected from M 87 in an explosion.

M 104 (NGC 4594), the Sombrero galaxy, is a ninth-magnitude spiral galaxy seen edge-on as an elliptical patch of light. Large telescopes, and long-exposure photographs, show a line of dark dust crossing the galaxy; this gives the galaxy a fanciful resemblance to a sombrero hat — hence its popular name.

Volans the flying fish

A faint constellation of the deep southern sky, introduced under the name of Piscis Volans by Bayer. The constellation represents the flying fish found in tropical seas. Its brightest star, Beta Volantis, is only of magnitude 3·7.

Objects of interest
Gamma Volantis is a pair of cream and yellow stars of magnitudes 3·9 and 5·8, easily seen through small telescopes.
Epsilon Volantis is a blue-white star of magnitude 4·5 with an eighth-magnitude companion visible through small telescopes.

Vulpecula the fox

A faint and elongated constellation at the head of Cygnus. Hevelius introduced it on his star map under the title 'Vulpecula cum Anser', the fox and goose, which has since been shortened. Although Vulpecula contains no stars brighter than fourth magnitude, the constellation is still of considerable interest. The first flashing radio star, or pulsar, was discovered within its borders in 1967, and the constellation has been the site of several recent novae.

Object of interest
M 27 (NGC 6853) is a large and bright planetary nebula popularly known as 'the Dumb-bell' because of its dog-biscuit shape. M 27 is reputedly the planetary nebula most easily seen through small instruments. Binoculars or small telescopes show it as a greenish eighth-magnitude patch covering one-quarter the apparent diameter of the full Moon.

M 27, the Dumb-bell Nebula, is a large planetary nebula.

Looking at
the Solar System

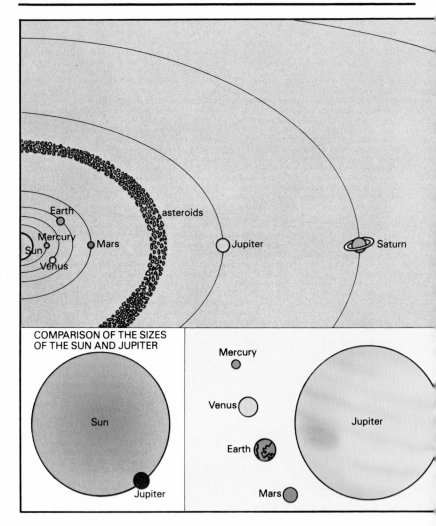

COMPARISON OF THE SIZES
OF THE SUN AND JUPITER

Sun

Jupiter

Mercury

Venus

Earth

Jupiter

Mars

Earth

Mercury

Sun

Venus

Mars

asteroids

Jupiter

Saturn

Planets of the Solar System in order of distance from the Sun (not to scale). Note that the orbit of Pluto crosses the orbit of Neptune.
Bottom: Relative sizes of the Sun and planets, shown to scale.

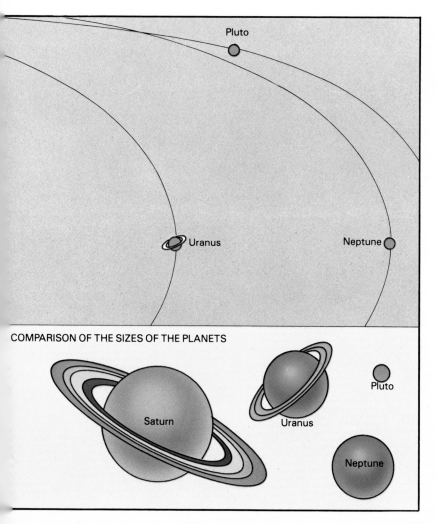

COMPARISON OF THE SIZES OF THE PLANETS

When ancient men looked at the sky, they saw several bright 'stars' that wandered around. They gave these wandering stars the name *planets*. Today we know that planets and stars are very different in nature. Whereas stars give out their own light and heat, planets shine by reflecting the light of the Sun. Planets can be made of rock and metal, like the Earth, or of gas, like Jupiter. There are nine known planets orbiting the Sun – Mercury, Venus, Earth, Mars, Jupiter, Saturn, Uranus, Neptune, and Pluto – plus a host of smaller pieces of debris such as asteroids, comets and meteorites. Together, these bodies make up what is known as the Solar System.

The Solar System is believed to have formed from a left-over disc of dust and gas orbiting the new-born Sun. In many cases, when a star

How the Solar System is believed to have formed from a cloud of gas and dust.

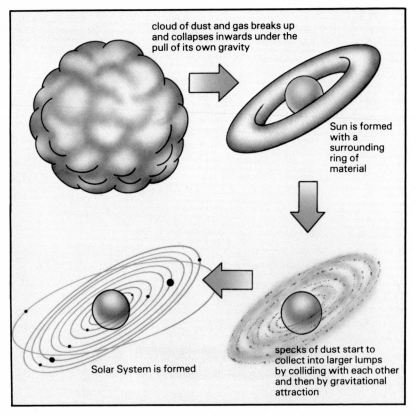

cloud of dust and gas breaks up and collapses inwards under the pull of its own gravity

Sun is formed with a surrounding ring of material

specks of dust start to collect into larger lumps by colliding with each other and then by gravitational attraction

Solar System is formed

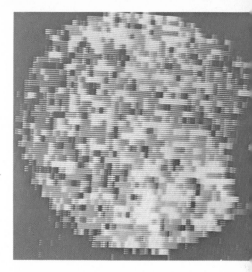

Sun photographed in ultraviolet light by the OSO 6 satellite. Each block of colour represents a different energy range on the Sun, from white (the most energetic areas) to black (least energetic).

forms, as described previously, the shrinking gas blob may split into two, producing a close double star. In other cases, two separate stars in a cluster may become linked by gravity, forming a wide double star. Still other stars may be left with a ring of material from which a planetary system forms. About one star in ten has no detectable stellar companion, and astronomers speculate that these stars may be accompanied by planets. But these planets would be too faint to see with existing telescopes.

Astronomers now think our own planetary system formed in the following way, which may also have occurred around numerous other stars. Specks of dust in the cloud around the new-born Sun began building up into larger, solid lumps, firstly by colliding with each other and then by gravitational attraction to other lumps. This 'sweeping-up' process continued for millions of years until the planets were formed, with gas from the cloud making up their atmospheres. The inner rocky planets – Mercury, Venus, Earth and Mars–have since lost their 'primeval' atmospheres. In the case of Venus, Earth, and Mars, these atmospheres have been replaced by new ones made from gases exhaled from the planets' interiors through volcanoes. But in the cooler outer regions of the

Solar System, giant planets were formed, made mostly of gas – Jupiter, Saturn, Uranus, and Neptune. These gas giants retain much the same atmosphere they had when they were 'born'.

The Sun

At the centre of the Solar System is its parent star, the Sun. We know that the Sun is a typical star, glowing due to the energy produced by nuclear reactions at its core. The Sun's diameter is 1·4 million kilometres, 109 times the size of Earth, which places it roughly midway in size between a red giant and a white dwarf. The Sun is the only star whose surface we can study in any detail, and you can make your own observations with even the smallest telescope. But here comes a most important warning: **It is dangerous to look at the Sun with the naked eye and you must never look directly at the Sun through any form of optical instrument or you will immediately be blinded**. The only safe way to look at the Sun is to project its image on to a white card. If you wish, you can attach a rod to the telescope to hold the card. Such a projection system has the advantage that several people can observe the Sun's image simultaneously.

To view the Sun safely, project its image on to a piece of white card. **Never** look directly at the Sun through a telescope.

The surface of the Sun

What will you see? Probably there will be several dark spots on the Sun's brilliant surface. These sunspots are areas of cooler gas. Whereas the Sun's visible surface, known as the *photosphere* (sphere of light) has a temperature of about 6000°C, sunspots are about 4500°C. They appear dark by contrast with their much brighter surroundings. Sunspots are darkest at the centre, the *umbra*, and are surrounded by a lighter *penumbra*. No one is certain exactly how sunspots form, but they seem to be associated with strong magnetic fields in the Sun. Apparently the magnetic field

telescope

Sun's image

card

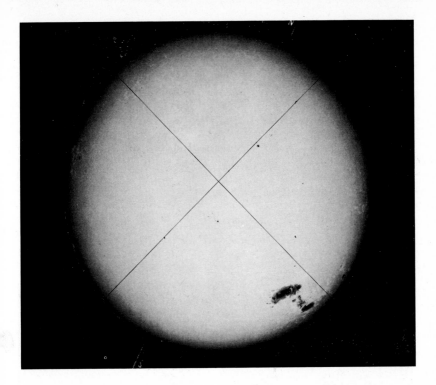

Massive sunspot group of April 1947. The two dark lines are cross-hairs in the telescope, used for measurement purposes.

prevents heat from reaching that part of the Sun's surface, causing the cooler spot.

Each sunspot lasts a few days or weeks, changing in size and intensity during that time. The number of sunspots rises and falls in a cycle lasting about 11 years on average. At sunspot maximum, as last happened in 1980, up to 100 spots of all sizes may be visible at a time. But at sunspot minimum the entire disc may be free of blemishes for days on end.

Sunspots range in size from small 'pores' 1500 kilometres across to enormous groups that would stretch halfway from the Earth to the Moon. Sometimes, bright eruptions known as flares occur near sunspots, particularly at the time of solar maximum. A flare lasts a few hours, blasting out atomic particles that may cause atmospheric effects on Earth such as aurorae and radio blackouts.

Watching sunspots cross the face of the Sun shows that the Sun does not rotate as a solid body. At the equator it spins once every 24·7 days, but this falls to once every 34 days near the

161

Above: Colourful aurora seen in the southern hemisphere, caused as atomic particles shooting out from the Sun interact with the Earth's upper atmosphere.

Above: Inner part of the Sun's corona, plus some bright prominences, seen at the total solar eclipse of March 7, 1970.

poles. The average rotation period of the Sun is taken as 25·4 days. But, seen from the Earth, the Sun takes 27·3 days to rotate (the *synodic period*), because the Earth is moving around the Sun in the same direction as it spins.

Closer inspection of the photosphere through large telescopes shows that it has a mottled appearance, like rice grains. This mottling, or *granulation*, is caused by convection cells of hot gas about 1000 kilometres across rising to the surface like water boiling in a pan.

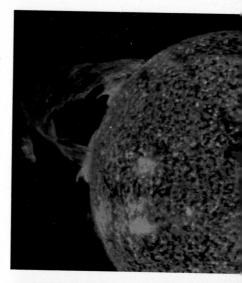

Right: Massive solar prominence, 600 000 km across, seen from the Skylab space station in 1973.

Surrounding the photosphere is a thinner layer of gas called the *chromosphere* (colour sphere). The chromosphere is visible only through special instruments, or at total eclipses when light from the brilliant photosphere is blotted out. The chromosphere appears pinkish-red in colour, which is the reason for its name. The colour is produced by light emitted from hydrogen atoms. The chromosphere is about 3000 kilometres deep, but through it to a height of 15 000 kilometres jut jets of hot gas or *spicules*, giving the Sun's edge the appearance of a flaming forest.

Larger protruberances seen at the edge of the Sun are *prominences*. Some of them are shaped like giant arches, consisting of hot gas looping along lines of magnetic force, often bridging sunspots. Other prominences are caused as flares eject clouds of gas into Space.

The Sun is enveloped in a faint halo or *corona* which, like the chromosphere, can be seen only when the bright photosphere is blotted out by special instruments or at eclipses. The corona consists of very thin gas, at a temperature of several million degrees, which glows with a pearly light. The corona streams outwards in fans and rays, but its shape changes from solar maximum to solar minimum,

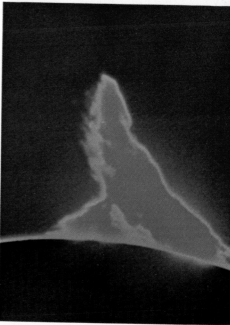

Right: Solar flare seen erupting at the Sun's edge, flinging off atomic particles that reach the Earth to cause aurorae.

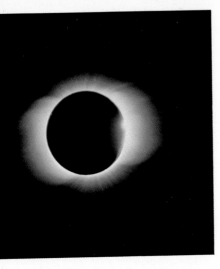

from the corona flows outwards through the Solar System, forming the so-called solar wind of atomic particles. One could say that the planets, Earth included, lie within the tenuous outer layers of the Sun's atmosphere.

Eclipses

Solar eclipses

Occasionally, the Sun, Moon, and Earth line up, causing an eclipse. The Sun is eclipsed when the Moon passes in front of it. By chance, the Sun and Moon appear in the sky as almost exactly the same size, so the Moon

being more irregular at sunspot minimum when activity is concentrated towards the Sun's equator. There is no outer boundary to the corona. Gas

Below: Total and annular solar eclipses.

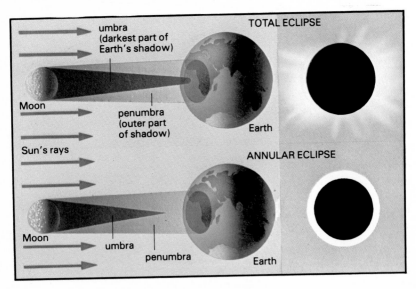

neatly blocks off light from the Sun's photosphere to produce a total solar eclipse. Immediately before and after totality, observers see the effect known as 'Baily's beads' (after the English astronomer Francis Baily, 1774-1844, who described them), caused when slivers of sunlight shine through the rugged mountains and valleys around the Moon's edge. During totality itself, which can last as long as seven minutes but is usually much less, the faint chromosphere and corona around the Sun are easily visible.

Totality at an eclipse is seen from an area covering only a small part of the Earth, because the Moon's shadow projected on the Earth is relatively narrow (no more than 300 kilometres wide). But a partial eclipse is visible over a much wider area. On some occasions, when the Moon is at the farthest part of its elliptical-shaped orbit from Earth, it appears just too small to cover the Sun's photosphere, thereby leaving a ring of sunlight visible as it moves between us and the Sun. This is called an *annular* eclipse, from the Latin word annulus, meaning a ring (annular eclipses do not occur annually!). There are on average about two total or partial solar eclipses visible from somewhere on Earth each year.

Total lunar eclipse. The Earth's shadow has turned the Moon a deep coppery colour.

less scientific value. A lunar eclipse occurs when the Moon enters the shadow of the Earth, and the eclipse is visible in any place on Earth where the Moon is above the horizon. Usually the Moon continues to shine a dull, coppery colour even when deep within the Earth's shadow, because some light is refracted through the Earth's atmosphere on to the Moon. But on some occasions, particularly when the upper atmosphere is very dusty, the eclipsed Moon can totally disappear.

Lunar eclipses

Total solar eclipses are important to astronomers because they allow the Sun's faint outer regions to be studied. Eclipses of the Moon are of far

Tides

The Sun and Moon have another important joint effect on Earth, and

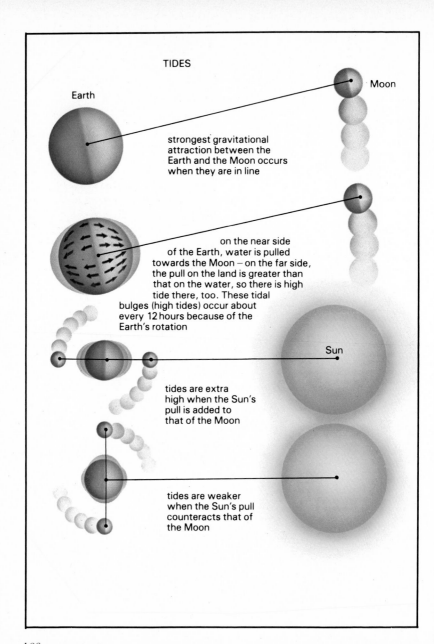

TIDES

Earth

Moon

strongest gravitational
attraction between the
Earth and the Moon occurs
when they are in line

on the near side
of the Earth, water is pulled
towards the Moon – on the far side,
the pull on the land is greater than
that on the water, so there is high
tide there, too. These tidal
bulges (high tides) occur about
every 12 hours because of the
Earth's rotation

Sun

tides are extra
high when the Sun's
pull is added to
that of the Moon

tides are weaker
when the Sun's pull
counteracts that of
the Moon

that is to cause tides by their gravitational pull. Because the Moon is much closer to us than is the Sun, its tide-raising force is greater. When the Sun and Moon pull in line (at new and full Moon), tides are particularly high. These are called *spring tides*. When the Sun and Moon pull at right angles, their effects partly cancel each other and the tides are then not so pronounced. These are known as *neap tides*, from an ancient word meaning scanty.

The Earth's gravitational pull has its own effect on the Moon. The Earth's pull has braked the Moon's rotation on its axis so that the Moon keeps one face permanently turned towards us – that is, it has a *captured rotation*. Several moons of other planets have also had their rotations locked-on to their parent planets in the same way.

The Moon

The Moon is the Earth's natural satellite. It is an airless, waterless ball of rock 3476 kilometres in diameter, almost a quarter the size of the Earth, remarkably large in relation to its parent. Indeed, the Earth–Moon

Crater Copernicus, near horizon, seen from Apollo 12 in orbit around the Moon. Foreground crater is Reinhold.

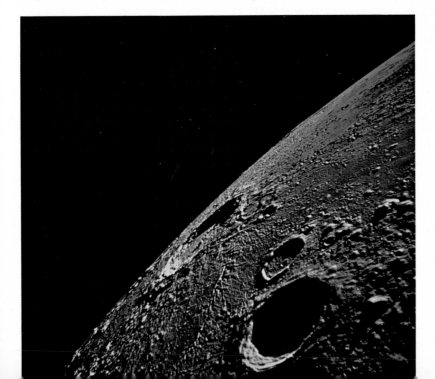

Sun data table

Average distance from Earth	149 600 000 km
Equatorial diameter	1 392 000 km
Rotation period	25·38 days
Mass	332 946 times Earth
Volume	1 303 946 times Earth

Moon data table

Average distance from Earth	384 400 km
Diameter	3 476 km
Rotation period	27 days
Mass	0·0123 times Earth
Volume	0·0203 times Earth

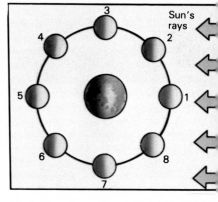

Above: Phases of the Moon depend on how much of its illuminated hemisphere is visible.

depending how much of its illuminated hemisphere we can see. A cycle of phases lasts 29·5 days, a length of time that is the basis for the month. A cycle of phases takes longer than one orbit of the Moon around the Earth, because the Earth is also moving around the Sun, and so the Moon has to move a little further around its orbit to return to the same position relative to the Sun.

You might think from the diagram opposite that eclipses of the Sun and Moon ought to occur at every new and full Moon respectively. But in fact the Moon's orbit is inclined at 5° to the plane of the Earth's orbit, so that only occasionally do the Sun, Moon, and Earth fall in an exact line to cause an eclipse.

The best time to observe features on the Moon's surface is when they are near the *terminator* (the dividing line between the illuminated and

system is sometimes described as a double planet. The Moon's average distance from Earth is 384 400 kilometres, making it a very close neighbour by astronomical standards. The existence of such a close and imposing satellite has undoubtedly influenced man's interest in astronomy and Space.

The Moon orbits the Earth once every 27 days, spinning on its axis in the same time, so that one face is permanently presented to us. As the Moon goes around the Earth it passes through a series of phases, from new, through full, back to new again

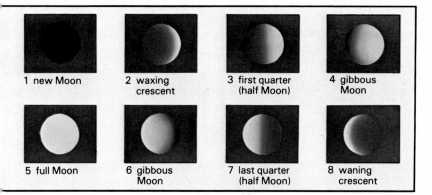

1 new Moon	2 waxing crescent
3 first quarter (half Moon)	4 gibbous Moon
5 full Moon	6 gibbous Moon
7 last quarter (half Moon)	8 waning crescent

Right: As the Moon orbits the Earth it also spins on its axis, so keeping the same face permanently turned towards us.

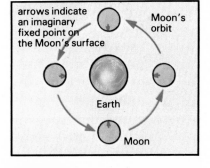

dark areas of the Moon), for they are then thrown into sharp relief by the long shadows. At full Moon, the details are washed out.

The surface of the Moon

A casual glance with the naked eye shows dark areas on the Moon's face, forming the familiar 'man-in-the-Moon' shape. Viewed through the smallest telescope or pair of binoculars, these dark areas are seen to be lowland plains. They are called *maria* (singular: mare), which is the Latin for sea, because they were once thought to be water-filled. We now know that they are composed of dark, volcanic lava that once spilled out from inside the Moon. The bright parts of the Moon are rugged highlands, pockmarked with craters of all

Right: Eclipses of the Moon occur when the Moon enters the shadow cast by the Earth.

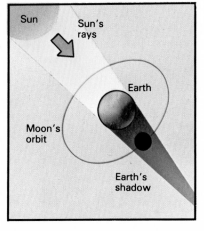

sizes. By contrast, the maria have relatively few craters on them.

Early lunar map makers gave the dark lowlands fanciful names, such as the Ocean of Storms (Oceanus Procellarum), Sea of Tranquillity (Mare Tranquillitatis), and Sea of Crises (Mare Crisium). Mountain ranges were named after formations on Earth, such as the Apennines, Alps and Carpathians. The craters were in

Moon photographed from Space by Apollo 11, showing parts of its near and far sides.

most cases named after scientists, although some other historical and mythological figures have crept in, including Atlas, Hercules, and Julius Caesar.

The largest craters on the Moon have diameters of 300 kilometres or more, large enough to swallow

170

Switzerland. Bright rays of ejected material fan outwards from some relatively young craters. The most prominent ray system extends from the crater Tycho, 90 kilometres across, in the southern highlands. Another prominent ray crater is Copernicus, 95 kilometres across, on the Oceanus Procellarum (Ocean of Storms). Closer inspection shows that Tycho and Copernicus, in common with many other large and prominent craters, have central mountain peaks and terraced walls. Other, older craters appear to have been flooded and partly demolished by once-molten lava from the maria.

Space probes have shown that the far side of the Moon is rather different in appearance from the near side, because it has no large maria, but is covered almost entirely with bright, heavily cratered highlands.

Above: Apollo 14 view across crater Parry to crater Bonpland. Smaller, sharper crater on their joining wall is Parry E.

Lunar exploration Controversy raged among astronomers for centuries about the origin of the Moon's features. One group said most of the craters were volcanic in origin, while the opposing faction held that they were scars of meteorite impacts. Exploration of the Moon by space probes and astronauts has confirmed

Below: Battered highlands on the Moon's far side, photographed from Apollo 14.

that the vast majority of lunar craters were caused by meteorites. Rocks brought back from the Moon by American astronauts in the Apollo programme show that the Moon's maria are of similar composition to the volcanic rocks on Earth known as basalt. One surprise was the extreme age of the lunar surface. Even the youngest samples, collected by Apollo 12 from the Ocean of Storms, are over 3000 million years old.

Analysis of the various Apollo Moon samples has shown that the Moon formed 4600 million years ago, at the same time as the Earth. Heat released during its formation produced a molten crust, which had solidified by about 200 million years later. Then came a bombardment of meteorites, as debris, left orbiting the Sun after the formation of the Solar System, was swept up. This bombardment, which other planets must also have suffered, lasted from 4400 to 3900 million years ago, digging out the great lunar craters and churning up the ancient crust. By 3800 million years ago, the interior of the Moon had heated up due to energy released by the decay of radioactive atoms, and molten lava flowed into the lowland areas, forming the maria. These lava flows ceased about 3100 million years ago. Since then, the Moon has been almost entirely inactive, apart from the occasional meteorite impact which blasts out a new crater, and a continual rain of micrometeorites which has eroded the lunar surface into dust.

But how was the Moon itself form-

Apollo 17 astronaut Harrison Schmitt is dwarfed by a broken boulder in a valley between the Taurus mountains of the Moon. Background hills are 8 km distant.

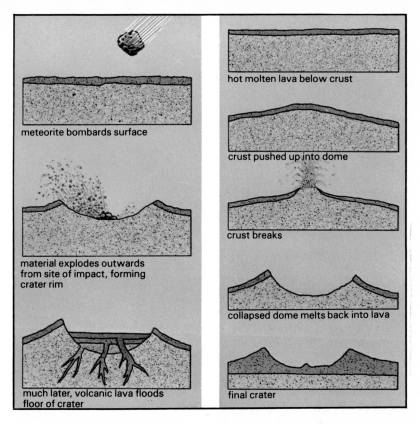

meteorite bombards surface

material explodes outwards from site of impact, forming crater rim

much later, volcanic lava floods floor of crater

hot molten lava below crust

crust pushed up into dome

crust breaks

collapsed dome melts back into lava

final crater

ed? Even the Apollo landings have failed to answer this question. There are three main theories about the origin of the Moon. One says it split off from the Earth; a second theory holds that the Moon was a passing body captured by the Earth; while according to the third theory, the Earth and Moon formed side by side, much as they are today.

The Earth and Moon seem to be sufficiently different in composition to rule out the idea that they were

Two ways of forming craters: by impact of meteorites, and volcanic eruptions.

once part of the same body. And it is difficult to see how the Earth could have captured as large a body as the Moon into the kind of orbit it has today. In view of these problems with the first two theories, the side-by-side origin of the Earth and Moon is the most popular one among astronomers today. But further evidence may change their views.

Planet data table

Planet	Average distance from Sun (million km)	Orbital period	Equatorial diameter (km)
Mercury	57·91	87·97 days	4880
Venus	108·21	224·70 days	12100
Earth	149·60	365·26 days	12756
Mars	227·94	686·98 days	6790
Jupiter	778·34	11·86 years	142800
Saturn	1427·01	29·46 years	120000
Uranus	2869·60	84·01 years	51000
Neptune	4496·70	164·79 years	49000
Pluto	5900·20	247·70 years	3000(?)

Looking at the planets

The two inner planets, Mercury and Venus, when viewed from Earth, never stray far from the Sun. Mercury is particularly difficult to spot unless you have a low, clear horizon, for usually the best times to see the planets are shortly before sunrise or after sunset, depending on the planets' positions in orbit. Venus is much more prominent, at its brightest shining more brilliantly than any other star or planet in the sky, and because of this it is frequently the source of erroneous Unidentified Flying Object reports! Venus is the object known popularly as the morning or evening 'star'.

Telescopes show that Mercury and Venus go through a cycle of phases,

Left: As seen from Earth, Venus presents a white featureless disc that goes through a series of phases on its orbit.

Planet	Rotation period	Mass (as a proportion of the Earth)	Volume	No of moons
Mercury	58·65 days	0·055	0·06	0
Venus	243 days	0·815	0·86	0
Earth	23h 56m 4s	1·000	1·00	1
Mars	24h 37m 23s	0·107	0·15	2
Jupiter	9h 50m 30s	317·900	1318·70	16+
Saturn	10h 14m	95·200	744·00	15+
Uranus	18h(?)	14·600	47·10	5
Neptune	23h(?)	17·200	53·70	2
Pluto	6 days 9 h	0·0025?	0·01	1

analogous to the phases of the Moon, as they orbit the Sun. The planets farther from the Sun than Earth do not show a cycle of phases, although Mars at times appears not quite fully round. Mars is a disappointing object when seen through telescopes because it is so small, and one has to await its occasional close approaches to Earth to see it well.

Jupiter, the giant planet of the Solar System, is unmistakably brilliant, second only to Venus. Saturn is less prominent because it is farther away from the Sun. Until 1781 the Solar System was thought to end at Saturn. But in that year, Uranus was discovered by Sir William Herschel during a telescopic survey of the sky. Subsequently, Neptune and Pluto were tracked down. Uranus is easily within the range of binoculars, and

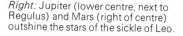

Right: Jupiter (lower centre, next to Regulus) and Mars (right of centre) outshine the stars of the sickle of Leo.

Neptune can also be found in this way. But Pluto requires a moderately sized telescope to detect it.

Mercury

Mercury is the closest planet to the Sun and has no moons. It is also one of the smallest planets, being only 50% larger than the Moon (exact details are given in the table on page 174). Telescopes show a disappointingly small disc with some dark smudges on it, like the Moon seen out of focus. Mercury is so difficult to observe that for many years astronomers wrongly assumed that the planet had a captured rotation, spinning on its axis in the same time as it took to orbit the Sun, 88 days. But radar observations in the mid 1960s showed that Mercury actually spins once every 59 days.

Astronomers were right in thinking that Mercury looked like the Moon. In 1974, the Mariner 10 space probe flew past the barren, rocky planet, showing it to be covered with lunar-like craters and maria. As airless and waterless as the Moon, and scorched by intense radiation from the Sun, Mercury provides no home for life. Occasionally, Mercury passes in front of the Sun as seen from Earth, an event known as a *transit*. When in transit across the Sun's disc, Mercury appears through telescopes as a dark blob, like a small sunspot. The last such transit of Mercury occurred in 1973. The next will occur on 12 November, 1986, and 14 November, 1999.

Mercury's surface is cratered like that of the Moon, as Mariner 10 showed in 1974.

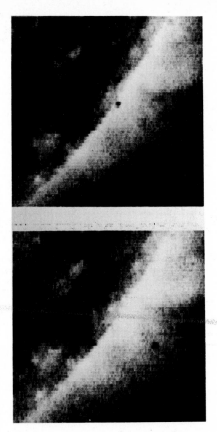

Mercury appears as a dark spot in these pictures of its transit of the Sun from a solar telescope aboard Skylab.

Venus

Venus, the second planet from the Sun, can come closer to Earth than any other planet. It was long considered to be Earth's twin because of the similarity in size of the two planets, but we now know that Venus is in its own way even more hostile than our Moon. Venus is such a brilliant object in our skies because of its nearness and also because it is entirely shrouded in dense, unbroken clouds which reflect most of the Sun's light. When Venus is close to Earth, binoculars reveal its crescent shape. Venus is so brilliant when seen through a telescope that it is best viewed against a twilight sky, to cut down dazzle. Like Mercury, Venus occasionally transits the face of the Sun, although even more rarely. The next transits of Venus will be on 8 June, 2004, and 6 June, 2012. The last were in 1874 and 1882.

Observers using telescopes often report dusky Y-shaped markings in the planet's clouds around the equatorial region, and brighter polar clouds. Photographs from space probes have shown that these markings do exist. The clouds of Venus spiral away from the equator to the planet's north and south poles.

Because we are unable to see the planet's surface, the rotation period of Venus was unknown until measurements were made by radar in the 1960s. Venus turns out to be doubly remarkable. First, it takes longer to spin on its axis than it does to orbit the Sun (243 days against 225 days). And it rotates from east to west (clockwise) – the opposite direction to the Earth and other planets. Nobody knows why Venus should be so different.

Radar observations from Earth and from space probes have allowed astronomers to map the unseen surface of Venus. Venus has craters,

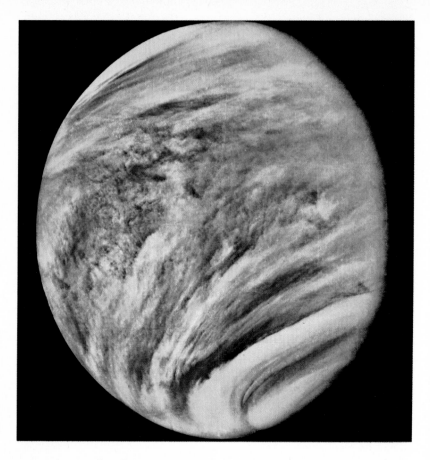

mountains, and valleys similar to those on Mars.

But what about the clouds and atmosphere? Russian and American space probes plunging through the atmosphere of Venus have discovered that it is composed almost entirely of unbreathable carbon dioxide gas, which bears down at the surface with a pressure 90 times the Earth's atmospheric pressure. The first

Swirling clouds of Venus, photographed by Mariner 10 in 1974.

Soviet probes to enter the atmosphere were crushed by this tremendous pressure long before they reached the surface.

Carbon dioxide traps heat like a very efficient blanket, building up temperatures at the surface to a furnace-like 475°C. To add to this

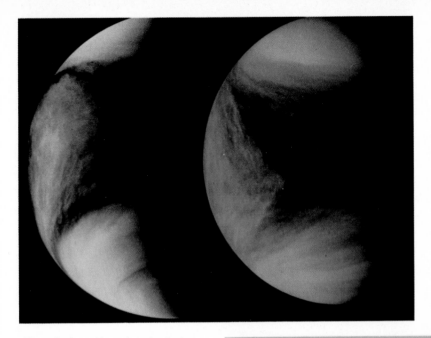

Above: Dark markings changing in the clouds of Venus, photographed on different days by a space probe.

hellish picture, the clouds of Venus are made not of water vapour, as are the clouds of the Earth, but of strong sulphuric acid. Despite its heavenly name and alluring brilliance, Venus is one of the most inhospitable places imaginable. Like Mercury, Venus has no moons.

Mars

Beyond Earth we come to the fourth planet in line from the Sun – the red planet Mars. As seen through a telescope, Mars presents a small orange disc, with white polar caps and dark surface markings that have

Above: Artist's idea of Venus rift valley.

been mapped and named in similar fashion to those on the Moon. The shape and intensity of the dark markings changes from season to season,

179

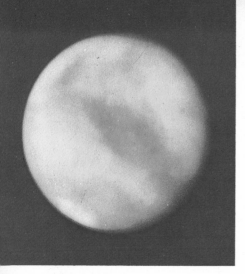

Above: From Earth, Mars shows a small orange disc with dark markings and white polar caps.

changes in surface markings.

This general impression gained by Earth-based observers has been extensively supplemented by space-probe exploration. In particular, we know that conditions on Mars are far harsher than previously believed, and hopes of finding life on the planet have been dashed.

The Mariner 9 space probe, which reached the planet in 1971, and two Viking spacecraft which landed there in 1976, showed that the carbon-dioxide atmosphere of Mars has the same density as that of the Earth's atmosphere at a height of more than 30 kilometres, so that it cannot retain much heat. Even on a warm summer's day near the Martian equator the air temperature does not rise above $-29°C$, and at night it falls

while the polar caps shrink and grow again. Occasionally, the surface of Mars is blotted out by dust storms in the planet's tenuous atmosphere, and these dust storms cause the apparent

Below: Part of the Martian rift valley system (caused by faulting of the crust) which stretches a total of 5000 km and is up to 70 km wide.

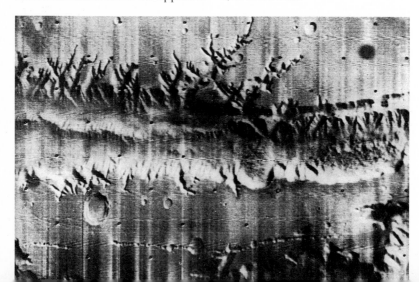

Artist's impression of a volcanic eruption on Mars as seen from the planet's surface.

to a frigid −85°C. Mars is locked in the grip of ice. Its polar caps are made of a mixture of frozen carbon dioxide and ice, and there is probably a permafrost shell of frozen water under the planet's rocky crust.

Mars is dotted with many craters, most of them apparently formed by the impact of meteorites. But there are also some enormous volcanoes. The largest of these, Olympus Mons, is the largest volcano in the Solar System, dwarfing even the volcanic Hawaiian islands on Earth. Mars also possesses a massive rift valley, similar to the Great Rift Valley of Africa. Much of the surface of Mars has been eroded by wind-blown dust. But conditions have not always been as cold and dry as they are now. There are signs of dried-up rivers on Mars, which perhaps flowed when the volcanoes erupted and pumped dense clouds of steam and other gases into the Martian atmosphere.

What of life on Mars? Some astronomers thought that the dark areas on the surface might be patches of vegetation, but space probes have shown them to be merely areas of darker rock and dust which change in size and shape as dust is blown around by seasonal winds. Of the legendary canals – long, straight lines which some astronomers reported seeing on Mars – there is no sign. These must have been optical illusions, caused as observers strained to see fine detail at the limit of visibility. The Viking Lander missions showed the surface of Mars to be a red, rock-strewn desert, with no visible plant or animal life. The red colour of the Martian rocks results from their high content of iron oxide

Rocky red surface of Mars photographed by the Viking 2 lander. Part of the spacecraft is visible in the foreground.

– known familiarly on Earth as rust! The Viking Landers incubated soil samples in their miniature on-board biology laboratories in search of life, but no Martian bugs or germs were detected. One day, astronauts will walk on Mars.

Mars has two tiny moons, Phobos and Deimos. These are believed to be captured asteroids.

Jupiter

Jupiter is the giant planet of the Solar System, 11 times the diameter of the Earth and weighing 2·5 times as much as all the other planets put together. Unlike the small, rocky planets from Mercury out to Mars, Jupiter is made almost entirely of gas. Its composition is mostly hydrogen and helium, similar to that of the Sun. Had Jupiter been 10 times or more heavier, it would have become a small star.

Jupiter is so large that it is clearly visible through binoculars as a disc. Also visible are its four brightest

age as they lose their gas and dust – this fate has befallen Encke's Comet. Cometary dust spreads out through the Solar System. When it is swept up by the Earth, it produces the streaks of light in the atmosphere called shooting stars or meteors.

Meteors

Meteors are specks of dust shed by comets and seen burning up by friction as they enter the Earth's atmosphere at high speed. On a clear night, five or six meteors an hour may be seen dashing at random to their fiery deaths. These are known as *sporadic meteors*. Typical meteors visible to the naked eye range between the size of a grain of sand and a pea. Meteors burn up at a height of about 90 kilometres, so there is no chance of being hit by one. As the meteoric particle plunges into the atmosphere and heats up, it leaves a trail of hot gas, which produces the sudden flash of light lasting a second or less that we see as a shooting star. The meteoric particle itself is too small to be visible.

At various times of the year, the Earth crosses the orbits of certain comets, encountering whole swarms of meteors. These form a meteor shower when meteors may be seen blazing into the atmosphere at rates of up to 60 meteors per hour. Unlike sporadic meteors, which appear to come from any direction at random, the members of a shower appear to radiate from a certain direction. The shower is named after the constellation (or sometimes even a specific star) from which the meteors appear to radiate – the Perseids radiate from Perseus, the Leonids from Leo, and so on. The apparent sources of meteor showers are called radiants.

A meteor shower builds up to a maximum of activity over several days as the Earth moves through the stream of particles. Amateur astronomers make useful observations of the number and brightness of meteors during the build-up and subsequent decay of the shower. Meteor observation is among the easiest branches of amateur astronomy, for it requires no special equipment, and can be very spectacular when a reliable shower such as the Perseids is putting on its

A Leonid meteor, photographed during the regular November shower of shooting stars.

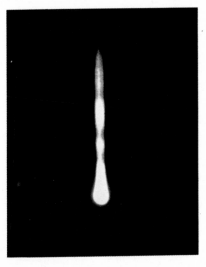

display of celestial fireworks.

By chance, the best meteor showers are most easily observed from the northern hemisphere. The year's brightest shower is the Perseids, when more than 60 meteors per hour may be seen under the best conditions around 13-14 August. Another bright shower is the Geminids. The year's most abundant shower is the Quadrantids, which radiate from a point in the north of Bootes, an area of sky once occupied by the now-defunct constellation Quadrans, the quadrant. But the Quadrantids are fainter than the Perseids, and their peak of activity is very short.

The table below gives details of the main meteor showers. Remember, though, that the estimated hourly rate applies to the best observing conditions, with the radiant high in the sky. If the radiant is close to the horizon, many meteors will be missed.

Major meteor showers

Name and approximate radiant point (right ascension and declination)	Date of maximum and Limits of visibility	Maximum hourly rate	Remarks
Quadrantids 15h 28m +50°	4 January 1-6 January	100	Many faint meteors.
April Lyrids 18h 08m +32°	22 April 19-24 April	12	Bright meteors.
Eta Aquarids 22h 24m +00°	5 May 1-8 May	20	Meteors with persistent trails.
June Lyrids 18h 32m +35°	16 June 10-21 June	8	Bluish meteors.
Delta Aquarids 22h 36m 00° and −17°	28 July 15 July–15 August	35	Double radiant.
Perseids 03h 04m +58°	13 August 25 July–18 August	68	Bright, flaring meteors, with trails.
Orionids 06h 24m +15°	21 October 16–26 October	30	Meteors with trails.
Taurids 03h 44m +14° and 22°	8 November 20 October–30 November	12	Double radiant. Bright meteors.
Leonids 10h 08m +22°	18 November 15–19 November	10	Erratic, somewhat unreliable.
Geminids 07h 28m +32°	14–15 December 7–15 December	60	Many bright meteors.

Left: According to the Steady State theory, new matter is continually created to fill Space as the Universe expands.

of the peculiar galaxies mentioned previously: radio galaxies, Seyfert galaxies, and quasars. The red shifts of these objects show they are exceedingly far away – well over 10 000 million light years distant in the case of many quasars. This means that their light has taken 10 000 million years or more to reach us, so we see them as they appeared long ago, shortly after the Big Bang is estimated to have occurred. According to one widely held view, quasars and their relatives are galaxies suffering violent birth pangs. After a few thousand million years the quasar settles down to resemble a normal galaxy. In other words, the Universe and the objects in it have been evolving in appearance, as the Big Bang theory predicts.

A further blow to the Steady State theory is that radio astronomers have heard what they believe is the 'echo' of the Big Bang. In 1965, the American physicists Arno Penzias (born 1933) and Robert Wilson (born 1936) detected faint radio noise coming from all over the sky. The discovery was soon confirmed by other astronomers. The reason for this radiation is that Space is not entirely cold, but has a temperature two or three degrees above absolute zero (the coldest temperature possible). This slight warmth pervading the Universe is interpreted as being energy (whose detectable radiation causes the radio noise) left over from the intense fireball of the Big Bang, and its existence is completely inexplicable on the basis of the Steady State theory. So important is the discovery of this radiation that in 1978 Penzias and Wilson were awarded the Nobel prize for the achievement.

Arno Penzias and Robert Wilson won the Nobel Prize for their discovery of what may be the 'echo' of the Big Bang, using this horn-shaped radio telescope.

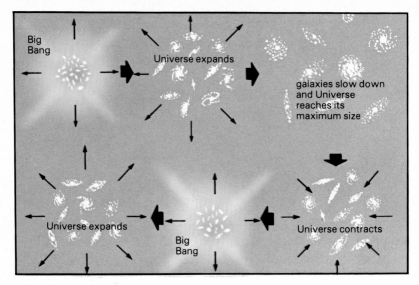

Big
Bang

Universe expands

galaxies slow down
and Universe
reaches its
maximum size

Universe expands

Big
Bang

Universe contracts

An oscillating Universe?

Oscillating Universe theory says that the Universe alternately expands and then collapses back to another Big Bang.

Another theory, a modification of the Big Bang, says that the Universe oscillates, alternately expanding and then shrinking again to another Big Bang. Thus there could be endless cycles of expansion and contraction, interspersed by Big Bangs, and the Universe could look very different in each successive cycle. On the oscillating Universe theory we would expect the current expansion of the Universe to slow down and eventually reverse itself, in the same way that a ball thrown into the air slows down and then falls back to Earth. But there is no evidence that this is actually happening. Astronomers have been unable to detect any slowing down in the outward motion of even the re-

motest galaxies. In addition, latest observations demonstrate that there is nowhere near enough matter in the Universe to provide the gravitational pull that would halt and reverse the outward motion of the galaxies.

Therefore it seems that the Universe is a once-only event. As we understand it at present, the Universe began in a massive explosion 10 000 to 20 000 million years ago: we can only speculate on the cause of this explosion. Since that time, the Universe has been expanding, and will continue to do so forever, slowly thinning out. One by one, the stars will die and in millions upon millions of years the Universe will become unimaginably dark, empty, and lonely.

Astronomical societies

There are two main astronomical societies in the United States.

American Astronomical Society, 1816 Jefferson Place, N.W. Washington, DC 20035
Astronomical Society of the Pacific, 1290 24th Avenue, San Francisco, CA 94122.

Various information relating to astronomy can be requested from these organizations, and also from local societies, observatories, and such planetariums as the Hayden Planetarium, Central Park West and 81st Street, New York, NY 10024.

Further reading

The following books contain a great deal of useful information for the practical amateur:

General
Calder, Nigel *The Violent Universe: An Eyewitness Account of the New Astronomy* (Viking, 1970)
Moore, Patrick *The New Concise Atlas of the Universe* (Rand McNally, 1978)
Muirden, James *Astronomy Handbook* (Arco, 1982)
Sky and Telescope (Sky Publishing Corp., 49 Bay State Road, Cambridge, MA 02238

Observer's Guides
Howard, N.E. *The Telescope Handbook and Star Atlas* (T.Y. Crowell, 1975)
Moore, Patrick *The New Guide to the Stars* (W.W. Norton, 1976)
Muirden, James *Astronomy with Binoculars* (Arco, 1983)

Research Projects
Greenleaf, Peter *Experiments in Space Science* (Arco, 1981)

Observatories
Kirby-Smith, H.T. *U.S. Observatories* (Van Nostrand Reinhold, 1976)

Glossary

albedo is the percentage of light that a body such as a planet or moon reflects. A body with an albedo of 1 is 100 per cent reflective; an albedo of 0 means the object is totally black.

altazimuth mounting is a simple form of mounting for a telescope or binoculars. The mounting allows the telescope to swivel freely up and down (in altitude) and from side to side (in azimuth).

aperture synthesis is a technique in radio astronomy that combines the output from several smaller telescopes to synthesize the view of the sky that would be seen by one large instrument. The dishes of an aperture synthesis telescope are usually arranged in a straight line.

aphelion is the farthest point from the Sun that an object such as a planet reaches in its orbit.

apogee is the farthest point from the Earth reached by an orbiting object such as the Moon or an artificial satellite.

astronomical unit is the average distance from the Earth to the Sun. It is equivalent to 149 597 910 kilometres.

background radiation is a slight warmth in the Universe, believed to be energy left over from the Big Bang explosion which marked the origin of the Universe. The background radiation, which is detectable at radio and infra-red wavelengths, shows that space has a temperature 2·7° above absolute zero.

binary star is a pair of stars orbiting around their common centre of gravity. Some binary stars can be seen to be two stars through telescopes, but others are so close together that their double nature becomes clear only when their light is analysed through spectroscopes; these are known as spectroscopic binaries. Some double stars close together periodically eclipse each other; these are termed eclipsing binaries.

black hole is a volume of space where the force of gravity is so strong that nothing can escape, not even light. A black hole is believed to form when a massive star collapses at the end of its life.

Cepheid variable is a type of star that periodically swells and shrinks in size, changing in brightness as it does so. The longer that a Cepheid takes to go through its cycle of light changes, the brighter it is.

conjunction is a close approach in the sky between two bodies. A planet is said to be in conjunction when it lies exactly behind the Sun as seen from Earth. In the case of Mercury and Venus, the planets nearer than Earth to the Sun, such an event is known as *superior conjunction*; *inferior conjunction* occurs when they lie between Earth and the Sun.

declination is a coordinate in the

sky, the equivalent of latitude on Earth.

Doppler effect is the change in wavelength of radiation from an object due to the object's movement towards or away from an observer. When the object is receding, the wavelength of the radiation is increased, moving towards the red end of the spectrum, so it is called a red shift. When the object approaches, the wavelength is shortened, causing a blue shift.

ecliptic is the path of the Sun around the sky each year against the background stars. It is so-called because eclipses occur when the Sun and Moon are near this line.

elongation is the angle between the Sun and Mercury or the Sun and Venus. At greatest elongation, Mercury and Venus appear at their maximum angle from the Sun.

equatorial mounting is a form of mounting for telescopes in which the axis of the mount is aligned parallel with the Earth's axis. By turning the telescope around this axis, the effect of the Earth's rotation can be counteracted so that the telescope points constantly at the object under study.

equinox is the moment when the Sun crosses the celestial equator. This happens twice a year, in late March and late September. At the equinoxes, the Sun is overhead at the equator at noon, and day and night are equal in length the world over.

globular cluster is a ball-shaped cluster of many tens or hundreds of thousands of stars. Globular clusters form haloes around galaxies. This includes our own Galaxy in which 125 globular clusters are known.

Hubble constant is a measurement of the speed at which the Universe is expanding. According to current measurements, galaxies move at about 16 kilometres per second for every million light years they are apart.

inclination is the angle of a planet's orbit to the plane of the Earth's orbit, or of a satellite's orbit to the Earth's equator.

inferior conjunction is the moment when Mercury or Venus are in line between the Earth and Sun.

Kepler's laws are the three laws of planetary motion discovered by the German mathematician Johannes Kepler. The laws say that planets move in elliptical paths; that they move faster when closer to the Sun; and that a planet's orbital period is governed by its distance from the Sun.

light year is the distance that a beam of light would travel in one year. It is equivalent to 9·45 million million kilometres.

Local Group is the cluster of about 30 galaxies of which our own Milky Way Galaxy is a prominent member.

Magellanic Clouds are two satellite galaxies of the Milky Way, appearing like fuzzy clouds in the southern hemisphere. They are both about 160 000 light years distant. The Large and Small clouds are about 0·03 and 0·005 the mass of our Galaxy respectively.

magnitude is a measurement of a star's brightness. Each magnitude step corresponds to a brightness difference of approximately 2·5 times.

main sequence is the name given to stars in the prime of their lives, burning hydrogen at their centres, as the Sun is now. When a star ages, it leaves the main sequence to become a red giant.

Milky Way is the faint band of light seen crossing the sky on clear nights. The Milky Way actually consists of distant stars in our Galaxy, and the name Milky Way is often used to mean our Galaxy as a whole.

neutron star is a tiny, compressed star left behind after a massive star has died in a supernova explosion. A neutron star is so called because it is composed of the atomic particles known as neutrons. A neutron star typically has the mass of one or two Suns compressed into a ball about 15 kilometres in diameter.

NGC is an abbreviation for New General Catalogue, a listing of star clusters and nebulae compiled by the Danish astronomer Johann Ludwig Emil Dreyer (1852-1926).

nutation is a slight nodding of the Earth's axis caused by the uneven gravitational pulls of the Sun and Moon. Nutation alters the tilt of the Earth's axis in space every 18·6 years.

object glass is the large light-collecting lens at the front of a refracting telescope.

occultation occurs when one body passes in front of another, temporarily obscuring it, as when the Moon occults a star.

opposition occurs when a planet lies opposite the Sun with the Earth in between.

parallax is the shift in position of an object against a distant background when viewed from two different places. The parallax of stars is measured by observing them at an interval of six months, ie from opposite sides of the Earth's orbit. The amount of an object's parallax reveals its distance from the observer.

parsec is a unit of distance, equivalent to 3·26 light years. One parsec is the distance at which a star would show a parallax of one second of arc.

perigee is the nearest point to the Earth reached by an orbiting object such as the Moon or an artificial satellite.

perihelion is the closest point to the Sun that an object such as a planet reaches in its orbit.

planetary nebula is a shell of gas thrown off by a red giant star at the end of its life. Through a telescope, such a nebula resembles the rounded disc of a planet, hence its name.

precession is the wobbling of the Earth on its axis like a spinning top.

proper motion is the change in a star's position with time, caused by the star's motion around the Galaxy.

pulsar is a radio source which gives out regular pulses of radiation. Pulsars are believed to be rapidly spinning neutron stars, which flash every time they turn.

quasar is a high-energy object far off in space. Quasars are believed to be the centres of galaxies in the process of formation. A quasar's energy source may be a massive black hole, which rips stars apart and sucks in the gas.

radio galaxy is a galaxy that emits strong radio energy, usually from lobes either side of the visible galaxy. These lobes are believed to be clouds of invisible gas ejected from the galaxy in explosions. Radio galaxies are related to quasars, many of which also show a double-lobed radio structure.

red dwarf is a star much smaller and cooler than the Sun. Red dwarfs are very faint.

red giant is a star much larger than the Sun, perhaps 100 times or more the Sun's diameter. Red giants are stars swelling up in size at the ends of their lives as they run out of hydrogen at their centres.

red shift is the increase in wavelength of the light from an object caused by the object's rapid motion away from us. This is also known as the Doppler effect. The red shift in light from distant galaxies has enabled astronomers to deduce that the Universe is expanding.

right ascension is a coordinate in the sky, the equivalent of longitude on Earth.

seeing is a term used to describe the steadiness of the atmosphere, which affects the quality of the image received during astronomical observations.

Seyfert galaxy is a type of galaxy (usually spiral) with a brilliant core, like a scaled-down quasar.

sidereal period is the time taken for an object such as a planet or satellite to complete one orbit relative to the stars.

solstice is the moment when the Sun is farthest north or south of the celestial equator, in late June and late December.

superior conjunction is the moment when Mercury or Venus is exactly behind the Sun as viewed from Earth.

synodic period is the time taken for an object to return to the same position in the sky as seen from Earth.

transit is the passage of a body such as a planet across the face of the Sun, as viewed from Earth, or of a celestial object such as a star across the observer's meridian (the north-south line in the sky).

vernal equinox is the moment when the Sun moves north across the celestial equator, on or around March 21 each year.

white dwarf is a small, intensely hot star about the size of the Earth, and left behind when a star like the Sun dies out.

Zodiac is the band of 12 constellations through which the Sun appears to pass during each year.

Index

221